# So You Have to Teach Math?

## Sound Advice for K–6 Teachers

MARILYN BURNS

ROBYN SILBEY

MATH SOLUTIONS PUBLICATIONS
SAUSALITO, CA

**Math Solutions Publications**

A division of Marilyn Burns Education Associates

150 Gate 5 Road, Suite 101

Sausalito, CA 94965

www.mathsolutions.com

The publisher would like to thank those who gave permission to reprint borrowed material:

Figure 7–1 on page 71 is reprinted from *About Teaching Mathematics: A K–8 Resource* by Marilyn Burns, © 1992. Published by Math Solutions Publications, Sausalito, CA.

Figure 11–1 on page 107 is reprinted from *Math By All Means: Money, Grades 1–2* by Jane Crawford, © 1996. Published by Math Solutions Publications, Sausalito, CA.

**Library of Congress Cataloging-in-Publication Data**

Burns, Marilyn, 1941–

    So you have to teach math : sound advice for K–6 teachers / Marilyn Burns, Robyn Silbey.

      p.   cm.

    ISBN 0-941355-29-2 (alk. paper)

    1. Mathematics—Study and teaching (Elementary)  I. Silbey, Robyn.  II. Title.

QA135.5 .B839775  2000

372.7'044—dc21

                    00-058222

Editor: Toby Gordon

Production: Melissa L. Inglis

Cover design: Leslie Bauman

Interior design: Angela Foote Book Design

Printed in the United States of America on acid-free paper

04 03 02 01    ML       3 4 5

# A Message from Marilyn Burns

We at Marilyn Burns Education Associates believe that teaching mathematics well calls for continually reflecting on and improving one's instructional practice. Our Math Solutions Publications include a wide range of choices, from books in our new Teaching Arithmetic series—which address beginning number concepts, place value, addition, subtraction, multiplication, division, fractions, decimals, and percents— to resources that help link math with writing and literature; from books that help teachers more deeply understand the mathematics behind the math they teach to children's books that help students develop an appreciation for math while learning basic concepts.

Along with our large collection of teacher resource books, we have a more general collection of books, videotapes, and audiotapes that can help teachers and parents bridge the gap between home and school. All of our materials are available at education stores, from distributors, and through major teacher catalogs.

In addition, Math Solutions Inservice offers five-day courses and one-day workshops throughout the country. We also work in partnership with school districts to help implement and sustain long-term improvement in mathematics instruction in all classrooms.

To find a complete listing of our publications and workshops, please visit our Web site at *www.mathsolutions.com*. Or contact us by calling (800) 868-9092 or sending an e-mail to *info@mathsolutions.com*. We're eager for your feedback and interested in learning about your particular needs. We look forward to hearing from you.

A DIVISION OF MARILYN BURNS EDUCATION ASSOCIATES

# Contents

*Chapters and Questions*   vii

*Introduction*   xiii

**One**   *Preparing for a Successful Year*   1

**Two**   *Planning Effective Math Instruction*   16

**Three**   *Leading Class Discussions*   32

**Four**   *Number Sense and the Basics*   42

**Five**   *Using Manipulative Materials*   51

**Six**   *Dealing with Calculators*   61

**Seven**   *Incorporating Writing into Math Class*   65

**Eight**   *Linking Math and Literature*   79

**Nine**   *The First Week of School*   83

**Ten**   *Connecting with Parents*   92

**Eleven**   *Handling Homework*   105

**Twelve**   *Preparing for Administrator Observations*   111

**Thirteen**   *Making Plans for Substitutes*   116

*Afterword*   121

# Chapters

# and

# Questions

**One**    *Preparing for a Successful Year*

1    What's the best way to get a handle on all the math I need to teach during the year?    1

2    What's important to know about the national math standards?    2

3    Since my instructional materials give me the direction I need for planning day-to-day lessons, why do I need to give attention to national or state standards?    4

4    What's important for me to think about when planning instruction?    6

5    How can I be sure that my instruction promotes students' learning?    7

6    How do I find out if units or specific lessons will be appropriate for my students?    8

7    How should I prepare students for the tests that the district or state requires?    9

8    Help! I'm switching from fifth grade to first grade. What advice can you give me?    10

9    Help! I'm switching from first grade to fifth grade. What advice can you give me?    12

10    Some of my students say they hate math. What should I do?    14

11    What field trips can I plan to help my students see math in action?    15

**Two**    *Planning Effective Math Instruction*

12    How can I structure my daily math period?    16

13    What kinds of questions best support math learning?    17

14    I know it's important for students to understand what they're learning. But sometimes I just want to tell them how to do something. Is this all right?    18

15    How can I assess my students to find out if they're learning what I'm teaching?   20

16    I'd like to try some one-on-one interviews to assess my students. How can I do this during class time?   21

17    What should I do if I plan lessons that are too hard or too easy?   23

18    I've heard that when assigning a problem, first you should have volunteers discuss how they might go about figuring it out. Doesn't this give too much away for the others?   24

19    What about cooperative groups in math class—do they really help?   24

20    How can I decide whether the best approach for a lesson is for students to work individually, with partners, in small groups, or as a whole class?   26

21    After I give my class directions for an activity, it seems that there's a flurry of hands from students who want assistance. What can I do about this?   27

22    Some students always finish assignments quickly. What should I have them do?   28

23    I spend an hour planning a classroom activity or assignment that takes my students five minutes to complete. How can I fix this picture?   29

24    It seems important to be organized and have all the details of a lesson planned beforehand, but I feel that I'm doing too much planning. How can I change this?   30

**Three**    *Leading Class Discussions*

25    How do I establish a classroom atmosphere that encourages students to participate in class discussions?   32

26    Are there general guidelines that can help me lead better math discussions?   33

27    What's a good way to introduce discussion guidelines to my class?   34

28    My students ask me why they have to explain their thinking all the time. How should I answer this?   36

29    Sometimes when I ask children to explain their thinking, they say, "I just know." Then what should I do?   37

30    I'm nervous that I won't be able to understand children when they're explaining their ideas. What tips can you give me?   37

31    Can't class discussions be too confusing for some students? I've seen struggling students who barely grasp one strategy and just fog out when others give their ideas.   38

32    I need help with responding to students when they give wrong answers in a way that won't turn them off from math. What suggestions can you give me?   39

33    How can I keep from calling on the same students all of the time? In class discussions, it always seems to be the same students who raise their hands to answer.   40

**Four**    *Number Sense and the Basics*

34    I hear a lot about students needing to know "the basics." What do the basics really include?   42

35    How can I help students memorize the addition and multiplication tables?   43

36    Should I use timed tests?   45

37    How much time should I devote to mental math?   45

38    I hear a lot about the importance of number sense. What exactly is number sense? How does it relate to basic facts?   47

39    Do you have any suggestions for assessing my students' number sense?   47

40    Can you really teach number sense?   48

**Five**    *Using Manipulative Materials*

41    What are manipulative materials?   51

42    How can I help parents understand why manipulative materials are important for helping their children learn math? I worry that they think we're just playing during math time.   52

43    What guidelines should I set with my class about using manipulatives?   53

44    What tips do you have for classes that have never used manipulatives for math before?   54

45    How often should I use manipulatives in my math teaching?   55

46    What about cutting paper into shapes—can't paper be seen as a manipulative, and a much cheaper one than wooden or plastic blocks?   57

47    How many different materials do I need? Can I start with just one or two materials?   57

48    I don't have enough of any material to use with my whole class. What can I do?   58

49    I know that manipulatives can help my slower learners, but do my better math students really need them?   58

50    I know that older students benefit from using manipulatives, but I worry they'll complain that the materials are too babyish. Do you have any hints for this?   59

51    What can I do for students who can do what I ask with the materials, but still have trouble with textbook work?    60

**Six**    *Dealing with Calculators*

52    Should I let my students use calculators? If so, when?    61
53    How can I best teach children how to use a calculator?    62
54    The students in my class bring their own calculators to school, so they all have different kinds. What should I do about dealing with the differences?    63

**Seven**    *Incorporating Writing into Math Class*

55    How can I get my students to explain their work and their answers in writing?    65
56    Is it useful for students to keep a math notebook, journal, or log?    66
57    Do you have any tips for managing students' math notebooks in the classroom?    67
58    I'm interested in examples of how teachers actually use math journals in their classes. Can you give some ideas?    68
59    What's a good system for keeping track of student work?    69
60    What about worksheets—when do you use these?    69
61    I've been pushing my students to write more complete explanations when they're solving problems. How should I react to their work?    70
62    Should I make notes when I read students' work so that I can remember what's important?    72
63    If I don't have time to give specific feedback to children's papers, isn't it okay, or even better, to indicate "good job" or "nice thinking" or some other general comment than to say nothing?    73
64    A friend has her students write letters to explain their reasoning so that they feel their writing in math class has a purpose. What do you think about this idea?    74
65    No matter how much practice my students have with writing, they still grumble and resist when I give a writing assignment. How should I respond to their complaints?    75
66    On some of the children's writing assignments in math, the spelling and grammar errors are glaring. Should I have students correct mistakes before I send their papers home?    76
67    What's a portfolio? Should I have my students create math portfolios?    77

**Eight**    *Linking Math and Literature*

68    Why is it valuable to spend math instructional time using children's books?    79

69    After I read a book to my class, there are always several children who want to borrow the book and take it home to share. How can I help parents use the book to its mathematical advantage?    80

70    I can see how children's books are appropriate for young children, but I teach sixth graders. What sorts of books work for older students?    81

**Nine**    *The First Week of School*

71    How can I find out how my students feel about math, and why should I?    83

72    Okay, I have a sense of how my students feel about math. Now what should I communicate to my students about math?    86

73    How can I find out what my students already understand?    86

74    What classroom guidelines should I set up at the beginning of the year?    88

75    Can you recommend favorite lessons for the beginning of the year that help establish and reinforce classroom guidelines?    89

76    Should I communicate with parents right away? If so, what should I say?    91

**Ten**    *Connecting with Parents*

77    How should I prepare for back-to-school night?    92

78    Should I prepare handouts to give parents on back-to-school night? If so, what should they be?    95

79    I know some of my student' parents dislike math. What advice can I give them so they don't pass their attitude on to their children?    96

80    Parents want to know how they can help their children, but some are afraid that they won't know how or will do the wrong thing. How can I address this at back-to-school night?    97

81    My students' parents are mostly concerned about the basics. How should I address this concern?    98

82    What should I tell parents about math homework?    100

83    A colleague told me that parents sometimes ask about "new math" and the question often brings snickers from others. What do they mean by "new math" and how should I respond to such questions?    100

84    How much math work should I send home?    102

85    Parent conferences are coming. What should I have ready?    102

86    How can I begin a parent conference? Should I ask parents what questions they have?    103

87    What should I say if parents want to know how they can help their child in math?    103

**Eleven**   *Handling Homework*

88   What are the purposes of math homework?   105

89   What options are there for dealing with homework that the children did the night before?   106

90   What should I do about children who don't do their math homework?   108

91   What should I tell parents about helping their children with homework assignments?   109

**Twelve**   *Preparing for Administrator Observations*

92   How can I plan for my principal's visit?   111

93   My administrator scheduled a visitation and we're in the middle of a unit and working on projects. I worry that the administrator won't see a "real" lesson. What can I do?   112

94   I want to show my administrator how much my students know. What's the best way to do this?   113

95   Is there anything I should avoid when my principal is observing me? If so, what?   113

96   I made my lesson plan for the observation before I knew where my kids would really be mathematically, so my revised lesson won't match the plan I gave my administrator. What should I do now?   114

97   What can I expect at the post-observation conference?   114

**Thirteen**   *Making Plans for Substitutes*

98   What can I do to set the scene for a substitute?   116

99   I worry that a substitute will have difficulty following my lesson plan or will confuse my students. Should I be concerned about this?   118

100   What are specific examples of learning activities that are good for substitute days?   118

101   How should I follow up with the class after being absent?   120

# Introduction

**M**ichele was twenty-one and right out of college when she got her first teaching job. The principal presented her with the districtwide curriculum guide for mathematics. When Michele looked over the concepts and ideas she was expected to cover in a year's time, she felt a sense of panic. "What's the best way to get a handle on all the math I need to teach during the year? What's important for me to think about when planning instruction? How can I structure my daily math period?"

Carmen had been teaching for seven years, all in first- and second-grade classrooms. She was reassigned and now faced teaching fifth grade for the first time. Math loomed as a new challenge that seemed both large and difficult, and she was worried. "I'm nervous that I won't be able to understand children when they're explaining their ideas. How do I find out if units or specific lessons will be appropriate for my students? How often should I use manipulatives?"

Brenda felt more confident about her teaching after her first three years, but her confidence didn't extend to mathematics. She had never felt successful in her own math learning, took the minimum number of math courses required in high school, and avoided math during college. "I worry that my own lack of interest in math shows. What should I communicate to my students about math? How do I establish a classroom atmosphere that encourages students to learn math?"

The journey of learning to become an effective teacher of mathematics includes grappling with questions like these. Most elementary teachers have the responsibility for teaching mathematics to their students and many teachers have questions, either about the math itself, how to teach it, or both. This book tackles the questions raised here along with many others. Whether you're a new teacher, a teacher new to teaching math, or a veteran teacher looking for a fresh perspective, the responses in this book are designed to give you direction and support for teaching mathematics well.

As with all teaching decisions, however, there are no clear-cut answers that work for everyone. The advice and guidance we offer you are based on the many years of experience we both have from teaching students, presenting inservice workshops, and providing in-classroom support to teachers. While we include examples of classroom lessons throughout the book, our goal is not to replace your instructional materials, but to illustrate the answers we are providing. We encourage you to tweak any of our suggestions so that they feel right for you and your students. The goal is for you to use our experience to help you develop expertise for teaching math with a teaching style that is uniquely yours and that fits the specific requirements and programs in your school and district.

Also, we know that while the answers we've presented represent our points of view, they don't take into account the realities of your classroom, your particular approach to teaching, or the specific pressures and needs that you face in your work. In order for *So You Have to Teach Math?* to be useful to you, you'll need to reflect on what we've written to decide how it can contribute to your thinking about teaching mathematics. We suspect there will be times when you don't agree with a particular idea we've offered or a pedagogical position we've expressed. In these cases, analyzing *why* you disagree can be as useful to you as analyzing why other sections in the book cause you to nod in agreement. Continuing to question and analyze our teaching practice is essential for all of us to grow as teachers.

A comment about reading this book: We don't intend for it to be read from cover to cover, but to be dipped into from time to time to answer specific questions that come up for you. To help you find a particular question, we grouped related ones into chapters. However, we ran into situations in which a question could fit into more than one chapter. In these instances, we've included references to other questions in the book to show you where you might turn for additional information.

A note to veteran teachers: We know that one of the demanding aspects of teaching is that novice teachers typically have the same responsibilities as do twenty-year veterans. A first year of teaching can be overwhelming. After a few years, we all learn how better to organize and manage classes, and teaching, in some ways, becomes easier. However, becoming better at handling the routines of teaching allows us to give more attention to issues of teaching and learning. You'll notice that some of the advice we offer in this book is targeted specifically at teachers new to the profession, offering tips for classroom procedures. If these questions don't meet your needs, skip over them, for we have also included information on teaching theories and practices targeted for more experienced teachers. We hope that there is plenty of help here for everyone, no matter your interests, prior experience, or particular challenges.

| One | Preparing for a Successful Year |

*Lydia and Samantha both taught fifth grade and wanted to be sure that their students were well prepared for attending middle school the next year. Their district had just published a new framework based on the national math standards, and the district testing program was new as well. Lydia and Samantha weren't sure how these changes should impact their math teaching. What was important to think about for their instruction? What preparation would the students need for the new test?*

*Janice had different questions about the upcoming year. She had been teaching fourth grade for five years and had just been reassigned to first. She liked math and knew the fourth-grade math curriculum well, but she hadn't taught first graders since her student teaching assignment. She felt she needed to get a handle on the year's goals and a better sense of what first graders could do.*

*Tom was concerned about another issue. This year he wanted to focus on his students' attitudes toward math. He worried about those students each year who seemed to have already come to hate math, and he wanted to think about what he could do for them. He was thinking about what sorts of field trips might help his students see math as relevant and enjoyable.*

*As these teachers' concerns demonstrate, there are many aspects to consider when preparing for a year of math teaching. Taking an overall look at them is valuable for identifying issues you want to be sure to address with your instructional program.*

## 1  What's the best way to get a handle on all the math I need to teach during the year?

Having an overall sense of where you're heading mathematically for the year is important. Each grade level has its own specific goals, and you need to look at the big picture of what students in your class should understand and be able to do by the end of the year. It's hard as a new teacher, or as a teacher new to a particular grade, to have a clear vision of this. You may have some memory about what it was like to have been a student yourself in the grade level you're teaching, but relying on your memory is risky. And, of course, your perspective was much different then. We recommend that you don't rely on just one source for looking at the math content for the year but that you take advantage of resources in several categories. Each will offer you a different perspective that will help shape your thinking.

One category of resources includes national and state standards. We know that these documents won't give you the help you need for planning daily lessons, but they can provide information about math teaching and learning that's valuable for seeing where in the larger picture your specific grade-level concerns fit. Also, national and state standards provide useful information for communicating with students and parents about what's important in learning math. (*See page 2–3 for a nutshell view of the national standards.*)

Next check your district guidelines about what your students should learn and the specific grade-level expectations. Districts use different names to describe these guidelines—math framework, curriculum guide, teaching and learning standards, student learning objectives, performance standards, and so on. It's also possible that your district hasn't compiled a specific document but is relying on the guidance of the state standards. Check with your district for a copy of your state standards, or check your state department's Web site.

A third category of resources includes the instructional materials provided by your district for teaching math. Especially if you're new to teaching math, these will probably give you the most help for charting the year's instruction. They outline lessons and help you gather your thoughts and prepare the materials needed for teaching. As you gain more experience teaching math, you'll probably do what most teachers do and supplement your instructional materials with ideas you've gleaned from colleagues, workshops, other materials, your own experiences, and feedback from your students about lessons you've tried.

## 2  What's important to know about the national math standards?

Our current national math standards, titled *Principles and Standards for School Mathematics*, are published by the National Council for Teachers of Mathematics. Released in April 2000, our standards are built on several important ideas:

- Learning math is essential for students.
- All students can learn mathematics, not just those with a "gift for math."

- Learning math means more than memorizing facts and performing procedures and includes thinking, reasoning, and applying skills to problem-solving situations.
- Students learn math by being actively involved in making sense of concepts and skills.

The document begins by addressing six guiding principles: equity, curriculum, teaching, learning, assessment, and technology. The rest of the document focuses on ten standards—five content standards and five process standards.

*Content Standards*

Standard 1. Number and Operation

Standard 2. Patterns, Functions, and Algebra

Standard 3. Geometry and Spatial Sense

Standard 4. Measurement

Standard 5. Data Analysis, Statistics, and Probability

The five content standards define the mathematics students must learn. They're the heart of what we teach. Although they're organized into five separate standards, it's important to remember that there are overlaps among the content areas. Number appears in all areas of math. Learning about measurement, statistics, and probability helps learning about number. Spatial sense plays an important role in patterns, functions, and algebra. The five standards together provide you a way to be sure that your math program is addressing the full breadth of mathematics that your students should know.

*Process Standards*

Standard 6. Problem Solving

Standard 7. Reasoning and Proof

Standard 8. Communication

Standard 9. Connections

Standard 10. Representation

While the content standards are the heart of the curriculum, the process standards are essential to keep it pumping. They describe the processes students use to learn and apply mathematics. In important ways, the two sets of standards are inseparable. The process standards provide the vehicles for bringing the content of the math curriculum to life and making it accessible to children.

Following a general description of each standard in the document are elaborations in four grade-level sections: K–2, 3–5, 6–8, and 9–12. These sections provide more specific information along with suggestions for classroom instruction.

## 3 Since my instructional materials give me the direction I need for planning day-to-day lessons, why do I need to give attention to national or state standards?

It's true that national and state math standards, and even your district standards, don't give you the specific planning help you need to face your students each day. But they do provide an overall structure of math teaching and learning that can guide your thinking as you make your daily instructional plans.

Think about when you plan to drive someplace you've never been. Specific directions help, and the more detailed they are, the smoother your trip is likely to be. But if the directions call for getting off at a particular exit or turning at a specific corner, and road construction requires an alternate route, you're better prepared when you have a broader sense of where you're going. In that case, it's also beneficial to have a general map of the area. In the same way, you can think of standards as broad road maps that provide a context for specific instructional choices.

When you make lesson plans, your attention to specifics is important for lessons to go smoothly. Making lesson plans calls for thinking through a variety of details—choosing the right materials, organizing the students, presenting directions, setting expectations for the students, providing for students who finish more quickly than others, and so on. However, along with working out these logistic details, it's also important to understand the key math ideas the lesson addresses and where these ideas fit into students' overall math learning. Standards can help with that.

Perhaps an example would be useful to illustrate these ideas. Empty the Bowl is an activity that you might enjoy trying with your students. We've used it with primary children as well as with older students. The activity gives primary children practice with addition, helps children develop their number sense, and provides a way to introduce them to ideas about probability. For older students, probability ideas and analyzing statistics become the focus of the activity.

Here's a plan for teaching Empty the Bowl:

1. Explain the activity: *Put 12 cubes or tiles into a small plastic bowl (such as a margarine tub) and then roll a die. The number on the die tells how many tiles to remove. Continue until the bowl is empty.*

2. Model with a volunteer how the students will work in pairs. You roll the die and remove the tiles; the volunteer student records the number rolled. To prompt the students' thinking, after each roll ask the class how many tiles still remain in the bowl.

3. Explain to the class that when only a few tiles remain, it's not necessary to go out exactly. If you roll a 5, for example, and only two tiles remain, you can remove them.

4. Tell the students that when the bowl is empty, partners should add the recorded numbers. With your volunteer, add the numbers for your game. Point out that if you went out exactly, the total will be 12; if the last roll was larger than the number of tiles left, the total will be more.

5. Before students pair up to work, ask: *What's the fewest number of rolls it would take to empty the bowl?* Discuss. Then ask: *What's the most number of rolls it would take to empty the bowl?* Discuss. List the numbers from 2 through 12 on a class chart and ask: *Is it possible to empty the bowl in all of these numbers of rolls?* Discuss, and have children give possible rolls that would result in each total number of rolls.

6. Tell the students that they are to play five rounds and then record with a tally mark next to the appropriate number on the class chart how many rolls it took on each round to empty the bowl. Record a tally mark for the game you modeled. If you think it's needed, model another game. *(See Figure 1–1.)*

7. Finally, tell the students that if time remains when they have played and recorded five tally marks, they should play more rounds and continue recording tally marks.

8. After all students have played and recorded, discuss the results on the class chart. Ask students how the class results compare to their individual results.

Empty the Bowl, along with providing numerical experience, provides the opportunity to introduce or reinforce several important ideas about probability and statistics:

Rolls to Empty the Bowl
2
3
4
5
6
7
8
9
10
11
12

**1–1.** Students use a class chart to record how many rolls in each round it took them to empty the bowl.

1. Some events are more likely than others, while some events are equally likely.
2. It's possible to measure the likelihood of events.
3. A sample set of data can be useful for predicting an outcome.
4. Larger sample sizes of data are more reliable than smaller samples.
5. Sometimes an experiment produces data that do not match a theory about probability.

The plans for Empty the Bowl ask students to consider several questions: Why are 2 and 12 the fewest and most numbers of rolls it can take to empty a bowl? Is it possible to empty the bowl in all numbers of rolls from 2 through 12? What do you think the data will show after all students record tally marks? Do you think it's more likely for some numbers of rolls to come up than others? Why? Suppose you had to go out exactly, so that if you had two tiles left and rolled a 5, you couldn't play. How would that change the results on the class chart? What would be the most number of rolls needed in this version? How does the larger sample of the class data compare with students' individual trials? The important ideas about probability and statistics in the previous list not only justify the activity but also guided the selection of these questions.

Thinking about important math goals can also help you think of extensions for your lessons. For example, you could have primary children repeat the activity with 20 items in the bowl. Older students could try the activity a second time using the rule of having to go out exactly and then compare the data from the two versions. You might think of other ideas to extend this lesson.

## 4  What's important for me to think about when planning instruction?

You should consider three aspects when getting organized for successful lessons: planning, preparing, and management. We realize that there are overlapping issues to these aspects, but we think it's helpful to think of them separately.

Planning first. We think of this more or less as a script for teaching a lesson. In order for lessons to run smoothly, you need to think about your presentation—the explanations you'll offer, the questions you'll pose to stimulate students' thinking, and the assignment you'll give to groups or individuals. It may help you to make written notes about the sequence of your lesson so you have an actual script that you can refer to during instruction. We do this often. (*See the instructions for* Empty the Bowl *on page 4.*) Reread your notes to check on the clarity of the explanations, questions, and directions. Do you think they're crystal clear? Will they promote reasoning?

Preparing next. While planning gives a lesson structure, preparing calls for thinking hard about the mathematics underlying the lesson. How does the topic connect to other topics the students have studied? What answers might the children give for the questions you pose? What responses might you have in mind to help their learning? The more thinking you do ahead of time about the mathematical content, the better prepared you'll be to maximize the benefit of the instruction. Still, no matter how carefully you prepare, expect—and hope for—surprises. Keep in mind that your role is to concentrate on understanding what children say, not to listen for answers you were expecting or hoping to hear. (*See page 37 for tips about listening to children's responses.*)

Finally, management. Tend to organizational details. If you're planning to use manipulatives during the course of the lesson, for example, have them on hand and ready for distribution before the lesson begins. If you want each group of children to have an assortment of pattern blocks, separate and organize them ahead of time so that distribution takes less than a minute. You may want students to make their own recording sheets. That's a great idea because students are not only recording the results of their math explorations but also learning how to organize their thoughts using a bit of their own style. If you need something to be duplicated, do it before the lesson begins. Make sure that the materials, supplies, and paper required for students to execute your lesson are ready to go.

## 5 How can I be sure that my instruction promotes students' learning?

We've learned to think carefully about the questions we ask in lessons to be sure that they promote thinking and reasoning and to make our learning goals clear to the class. Here's an example. Suppose you're planning a lesson to focus students' strategies for adding mentally—perhaps single-digit numbers for younger children or two- and three-digit numbers for older students. You want students to be able to compute accurately and efficiently. But your goals should also include helping them develop strategies that allow them to be flexible in their thinking and make computing decisions appropriate for the numbers at hand.

How might you begin such a lesson? You might write 6 + 7 on the board. Or for older students, *Our class has 27 students. Ms. Kringle's class has 28 students.* Then you could pose a problem: "How much is 6 plus 7?" or "How many students are there in our class and Ms. Kringle's class together?" But what typically occurs as a result of questions like these is that hands shoot up from the students who think more quickly while the others either struggle to think or merely wait for the more confident students to reply. Putting the initial emphasis on the correct answer can exacerbate this situation.

We have tried posing the question differently: "How can you find the sum of 6 and 7?" or "Who can explain why 6 plus 7 equals 13?" Or, for the older students, "What would you do to figure out how many students there are altogether in our class and

Ms. Kringle's class?" But from our experience, unless we talked with students first about what we expected, even these sorts of questions resulted in a scurry for the correct answer.

It's important before posing any question to help students understand your interest in how they think and reason. To this end, take a moment at the beginning of a lesson to explain your purpose. For instance, for the example above, you might say, "Today I'm interested in hearing how many different ways we can think of to add numbers in our head. I'm going to give you a problem and give you some time to figure out the answer. Then you'll have a chance to report your answer and also explain to the class how you thought it through." Another approach is to pose the problem and then say, "Figure out the answer and then check with your partner that you both agree. Then each of you should take a turn telling your partner how you figured it out. In a few moments, you'll have a chance to explain your thinking to the class so we can hear all the different ways of solving the problem."

After the students have had time to figure, and before beginning a class discussion, again set the guidelines. Remind the class that you're interested in how they thought about the problem. You might also tell them, "When someone reports, your job is to listen to hear if you figured the same way or in a different way." Remember, your students will do their best to give you what you ask of them, so make sure your directions and questions ask for the result you want.

While lessons like this may seem unusual to students at first, after several experiences they'll be more comfortable with your focus on thinking. They'll come to expect that they'll have to explain how they reasoned, and they'll get better at listening to others' ideas.

## 6  How do I find out if units or specific lessons will be appropriate for my students?

Whether you're thinking about a whole unit or a particular day's lesson, it's important to begin instruction by finding out where your students' learning can begin. The instructional materials you use may include some sort of formal preassessment. Even so, it's useful to learn from the class informally. Whether you're beginning a unit on addition and subtraction, multiplication, or fractions or planning a specific lesson on measuring length or classifying triangles, put up a sheet of chart paper with two headings: "What I Know About _____" and "What I Want to Find Out About _____." Inviting the class to contribute to the chart can help define where your instruction should begin. For example, your second graders may say that they know how to add, but they'd like to find out how to subtract large numbers. Or perhaps they know how to measure with a ruler, but they'd like to know how to measure the distance around a red rubber ball.

Tell the students that you'll use the results on the chart when planning lessons. Ask yourself, "What would I like my class to know and be able to do as a result of this instruction? How does this learning relate to what else they've been studying?" Share your goals with students in a way that they can understand. You may want to post them in the classroom, maybe on the chart paper of your students' ideas. Your students will benefit from knowing the goals you have in mind for them, and the goals send a clear message about your expectations for their learning. Also, when children see their ideas reflected in goals, they are empowered as participants in their own learning.

## 7 How should I prepare students for the tests that the district or state requires?

There's a wide variety of math tests that students have to take. Some include only multiple-choice items; some include questions that call for short written answers; some also pose problems that call for longer written responses. Whatever the form of the questions, your students should have experience with it beforehand so that they are familiar with the format of the test and how they are to respond. But rather than think about preparing students just before they have to take a test, think about preparing students for tests as an ongoing part of instruction.

Let's consider multiple-choice test items first. Try some hands-on-the-table math—no pencil, no paper, no writing. These are good starters for math class. Write a problem on the board that's similar to the kind of multiple-choice test item they'll face, listing possible answers as they'll appear in the test booklet. Then tell the students that for this hands-on-the-table problem, they can use only their heads and the ideas of others. Have them talk in pairs first and then ask for responses. Insist that the person answering give an explanation of how he or she found the answer. Always ask if anyone thought about it in a different way.

You might choose a problem for which the math is familiar to them, for example:

Ruby had 47 marbles in her collection. For her birthday, she received a box of 25 marbles. How many marbles does she have now?

    a. 22

    b. 62

    c. 72

    d. 81

Or you might choose a problem for which the math is new. Remember that many standardized tests include items that don't reflect what you're supposed to teach. These items appear on norm-referenced tests as a way to influence the curve of students' results. For example, fifth graders taking a test in late fall might encounter a problem that calls for dividing by a fraction, something they haven't learned as yet:

$3 \div \frac{1}{4} = ?$

a. $\frac{3}{4}$

b. $\frac{1}{12}$

c. $1\frac{1}{4}$

d. 12

Don't think about rearranging your curriculum for items like these. However, it can be useful to discuss with your students what they might do when they encounter something new and strange. The previous example presents an opportunity for students to think about what they know about division. Or they can think about changing an unfamiliar problem to a similar one that they can do and see if that helps. In this case, even students who haven't formally studied division of fractions can reason to arrive at an answer. By realizing that they can think of division problems with whole numbers such as $8 \div 4$, as "how many 4s fit into 8," they can think the same way for this problem and figure out "how many $\frac{1}{4}$s go into 3."

The goal for these hands-on-the-table exercises is to help your students get used to approaching tests with an attitude of reasoning and making sense of the questions. Mix up the practice to include questions of all the types your students will encounter. The good news, you can tell your students, is that when they take a test they'll have paper and pencil available to them, which can help with their figuring. The tough news, however, is that they won't be able to talk with one another, because a test needs to measure what each of them knows and can do. Reinforce for them that their job when taking a test is to give the best picture they can about what they understand, what they can do, and what they haven't learned yet. This information helps teachers better plan how to help them learn.

Tests can be stressful for students, more for some than for others. Tests are also stressful for teachers, as we sometimes feel they measure our success as well. If you're anxious about the test, don't communicate your anxiety to your students. Instead, let your students know that the test is their opportunity to show their stuff and encourage them to do the best they can.

## 8    Help! I'm switching from fifth grade to first grade. What advice can you give me?

If you're used to working with older students, changing to first grade will certainly require some adjustments. A year's growth can make an enormous difference in a child, and this growth compounded over several years calls for thinking about the classroom in very different ways. From our own teaching experiences, however, we've learned that changing grade levels has been tremendously helpful for expanding—and improving—our teaching skills. It's understandable for the change in your teaching assignment to produce some anxiety, but we urge you to embrace the change with curiosity and enthusiasm. You'll be a better teacher for it. Here are some pointers for thinking about the differences between the two grades—both about the children and about the mathematics they study.

One difference is that things in first grade generally require more time than you're accustomed to spending with older students. Writing, for example, is a newly learned skill for young children. Holding a pencil is tough for some children, and the time and labor required for their written work may surprise you. After some experience, however, you'll learn how to predict more accurately the amount of time needed for a particular activity.

In terms of their mathematical ability, children's most evident skill at this age is their ability to count. They count on counting. While our goal is to help children move beyond counting and learn to reason numerically, at this age counting is their safety net, a skill they've learned to trust. You may notice that children's counting ability typically surpasses their understanding. Some children are able to count to one hundred or higher, but while they've learned the *pattern* for counting, they don't understand the *structure* of the numbers—that 67, for example, represents six 10s and seven 1s. At times, of course, fifth graders may resort to counting when they figure, but they also have other strategies available to them and have internalized relationships among numbers that aren't yet available to younger children.

There are also many specifics that young children haven't yet learned. Along with possessing limited writing skills, they're probably not reading well enough for you to rely on written directions. Their vocabulary is limited and they may not know what it means for something to be "twice as much." You'll need to review and reinforce the meaning of words—for example, *same* and *different*—and give children many experiences using them in contexts. They also most likely can't tell time or count the value of coins.

Here's a classroom example that may give you insights into differences between first and fifth graders. A class of first graders was investigating the number of cubes in a handful. The teacher modeled how to take a handful—reaching in with one hand, gathering cubes with it, holding it with her fist down, and shaking it twice to get rid of extra cubes. Each child came up and took a handful, then went back to his or her desk to snap the cubes into a train, count them, and write the number he or she had on a three-by-three-inch Post-it. Then the teacher helped the children organize the Post-its into a class graph. All this took quite a bit longer than it would have with fifth graders!

"How many cubes do you think there are in our handfuls altogether?" the teacher asked. Most of the children raised a hand to respond. But when the teacher asked the children to explain their predictions, most shrugged or simply said, "I just guessed." The guesses ranged from twenty to "a jillion, billion." The teacher then asked that each group of four students figure out the number of cubes in their handfuls combined. "Put the cubes at your table together into trains of 10. Then be ready to tell how many 10s and how many extras you have." One table had eight extra cubes and figured out that they needed two more to make another 10. The teacher polled the other groups to see who had two extras to offer them. In this way, she helped groups make as many 10s as possible. She had the children bring the 10s up to the chalkboard tray. She modeled how to count the 10s, then the extras, and record the total.

"Suppose we put our cubes into trains with five cubes in each instead of ten," she said. "Then we could count by 5s. Would this give us the same total number of cubes?" While this answer would be obvious to fifth graders, in this first-grade class, it was a pretty even split between those who responded yes and those who thought no. Also, while it would seem obvious to fifth graders that you could make trains of five merely by breaking each train of ten in half, this was a new discovery for the young children.

You'll learn about the many differences between the two grades in short order. Rely on your instructional materials, on the advice of colleagues with more experience with young children, and on paying close attention to the children themselves. Listen to them talk, and watch them at work and at play.

## 9   Help! I'm switching from first grade to fifth grade. What advice can you give me?

We recommend that you first read the advice we give in the previous section for teachers in the opposite situation—those moving from fifth grade down to first (*see page 10*). This will introduce you to some of the differences between these grade levels that we think are important. Especially pay attention to the classroom example we offered about handfuls of cubes. You can probably imagine the lesson we described with younger children, or you may have taught a similar lesson yourself. Following is how the same lesson was used to meet the needs of fifth graders. The contrast can help illustrate more of the differences.

As the first-grade teacher had done with her class, the fifth-grade teacher modeled for the students how to take a handful of cubes—some organizational tips work in all grades! The students recorded their totals on Post-it Notes that they then organized into a graph. When the teacher asked how many cubes the students thought were in their handfuls altogether, the fifth graders didn't make wild guesses. They reasoned numerically and were able to support their estimates, explaining how they thought about the total in relation to the number of cubes individual students had.

The teacher also asked the students to figure out how many cubes were in their group of four students, but asked them to figure in their heads and leave their individual trains intact. This not only gave the students practice with calculating mentally but also left the trains available for the investigation to come. The teacher recorded the groups' totals on the board and had the class add the numbers, again giving them practice with calculating.

Finally the teacher began a discussion of averages. The students had been introduced to the three kinds of average—*mean*, *median*, and *mode*—and this experience presented another opportunity for them to think about these ideas. It was easy for them to identify the mode by seeing which column on the graph had the most Post-its. Then they talked about lining up all of their trains from smallest to largest to see which train was in the middle of the line and, therefore, was the median. They made predictions first from looking at the graph and then they actually lined up their trains in size order on the floor in front of the chalkboard, placing them on their sides to avoid the distraction of toppling trains. They then talked about figuring the mean by dividing the total number of cubes by the number of students—another chance for calculating mentally. Finally, to make the idea of mean concrete, they "evened out" the trains on the floor, taking cubes from the longer trains and adding them to shorter ones until most of the trains were the same length and a few were just one cube shorter. They compared this to the mean they had calculated.

Fifth graders are more capable than first graders in many ways. Ideas about smaller numbers that are new concepts for first graders will be obvious to fifth graders. Fifth graders, for example, know that if twenty-five children line up in pairs, one child won't have a partner. They most likely will explain that 25 is an odd number, or that there will be twelve pairs and one extra. First graders, however, would need to figure this out in some way. They don't know about odd and even numbers, or if they do, they probably wouldn't apply what they know to this context. If they thought about the problem, they'd benefit from actually lining up to verify their thinking in a real way; fifth graders wouldn't need verification for a problem like this.

There are several different challenges in the upper grades. The mathematics in the fifth-grade curriculum is more extensive and demanding. If, for instance, you're not confident about the ideas of mean, median, and mode, you may have some studying to do. While this can be daunting, take it as an opportunity to expand your own mathematical understanding. Seek help from colleagues if you need to, learn from the instructional materials, and keep an inquiring attitude toward all that you have to teach. And, as we advised for the opposite switch, pay close attention to the children themselves at work and at play. They'll be your best guides for making the change.

## 10 Some of my students say they hate math. What should I do?

First of all, let's look at why students say they hate math. As a rule, we're uncomfortable in situations in which we lack understanding and feel somehow deficient. It's the same with children. They "hate" math when they haven't been successful learning it, don't think they can learn it, and feel powerless. While math won't be the favorite subject of all students, most probably wouldn't say they *hated* it if they experienced success.

There are other possible reasons that students may say they hate math. Some children have been influenced by their peers or family members and feel that hating math is a cool thing to express. We've heard children say, "My dad hates math, too," or, "All the kids hate math," or, "My brother isn't any good in math either."

We recently spotted an ad in a major popular magazine that showed a full-page photo of a boy with a look of despair holding his face in his hands. The headline read: *Wipe that "I hate fractions" look off his face in less than 15 minutes.* The solution? A recipe for S'mores, a gooey treat made with marshmallows and chocolate. Ah, if it were only that easy to address math aversion!

Whatever the source of the problem, what can you do? First, it's important to acknowledge these feelings and not dismiss them, no matter their origin. We're all different and, therefore, we like different things. While some students really do enjoy the challenge of math, others get excited by learning topics in science or social studies, and others are voracious readers who feel that learning math is an annoying interruption. But although students have favorites, they still need to do their best to learn all of what they're presented with in school. It's not productive for them to carry a negative attitude toward something that is and will continue to be such a big part of their lives.

While this sort of acknowledgment is helpful, it probably won't do much by itself to change attitudes. But it's an important start. At least students will know that you're aware of the situation, respect it, and will do your best to help them. Let them know that you'll do your best to help them see how mathematics can be accessible, interesting, and even enjoyable. For that to happen, children need math experiences that capture their imaginations and get them actively involved. The coin riddles we suggest in Chapter 9 are an example of such an activity (*see page 84*) and we've sprinkled lots of others throughout the book. It's not possible to make every lesson a "wow" experience for every student, of course, but as much as possible, students' math experiences should be engaging. We hope that many of the suggestions we've given in this book will help with this challenge.

When students are having trouble, the best approach is to work from their strengths and interests. Let them know that it's your job as their teacher to help them learn. They need to participate, of course, but they won't have to do it alone and you won't abandon them. The key to changing students' attitudes is success. Students who are competent in and confident with mathematics still may not choose it as their favorite subject in school, but success goes a long way in diminishing dislike.

## 11 What field trips can I plan to help my students see math in action?

Many teachers think of field trips as valuable experiences for students in a variety of ways but not often for enhancing their mathematics learning. However, getting out of the classroom for a mathematical purpose can give a boost to learning.

Math field trips don't have to be elaborate or costly. A hike around the school can be a problem-solving field trip. Tell your students to imagine that they have been asked to build a fence around the outside of the entire school and playground area and need to estimate the cost. Beforehand, clip a newspaper ad or make a telephone call to get the cost of fencing. Or have them estimate how far they walk going to and from the lunchroom, library, or gym each day, each month, and in the entire school year.

How about a field trip to a nearby supermarket for an investigation? For example, have your students research the validity of statements such as: "It's always more economical to buy the largest size of an item," "It's less expensive to buy frozen orange juice and add water than to simply buy the bottle of ready-made juice," and "The store brand always costs less than the name brand." Present these statements as examples and add students' ideas to compile a list. Then have students work in groups and choose one statement to investigate. After the trip to the store, students can analyze the results and report their findings to the class. Also, they could write a shopping guide for their families based on what they learned.

Not all field trips have to be centered around a mathematical investigation in order to involve students with mathematics. The organization of any field trip involves using mathematics, and you should invite students to help you with making plans. How soon after the beginning of school will you depart? What time will you return? How long will the field trip last? What costs are involved? Are they per-person expenses, such as admissions, or is there one large cost to be divided among all the participants, such as a bus? These and other questions will help your students figure the total cost per person.

| Two | *Planning*
*Effective*
*Math*
*Instruction* |

**R**honda *felt comfortable with the content of the math curriculum at her grade level, but she felt she needed to improve how she presented it. She used various approaches for planning lessons and had been working on learning to assess what her students knew, incorporating more activities into math instruction, and using cooperative groups. But she still had many questions. "When do cooperative groups make sense and when don't they?" she wondered. "How can I meet the needs of students who finish assignments quickly? What about those kids who always seem confused? What sorts of questions should I ask to best support learning?" Rhonda's concerns are valid. Her search for answers is the key to improving her teaching practice. It's a career-long pursuit, and improvement happens one year at a time.*

## 12  How can I structure my daily math period?

There's no single best way for all math periods to be organized. The organization depends on a myriad of conditions—the materials you plan to use, how you want the students to work, and the assignment you plan to give. Keep in mind that varying the structure of math lessons is a way to maintain interest and keep math classes from becoming humdrum.

That said, it's beneficial to think about the different ways you can organize your class for math learning and your expectations for the students in each situation. For example, there will be times when students will work with a partner or small group and other times when they'll work individually and not share ideas. In the first situation, it's appropriate for students to talk with one another, but that's not so in the second scenario. Also, there are times when students will use particular materials— manipulatives, scissors and glue, specific books, and so on. Again, guidelines should be clear. Whatever organizational structure you use, your goal is to present clear guidelines that the students understand so that they can switch from one setting to another with minimal disruption. Guidelines should address, for example, how to use and put away materials, whether students have to sit in a particular place or can pick a location, whether they will choose a partner or be assigned someone to work with, and so on. Establishing guidelines sets the conventions for working during class that can help lessons go more smoothly and can help you focus more on learning than on managing.

Some teachers like to prepare a binder of information for visitors who come to the class, whether they are parents, teachers from other classrooms, or other observers. The binder contains information about the class's educational program and also about classroom procedures and logistics. Teachers have included a variety of materials in their binders—portions of the district guidelines regarding learning and expectations, lists of topics that will be taught during the year, examples of assignments students will be expected to do, samples of student work, cartoons that communicate a useful or important message, and so on. Creating such a binder with your students is a way to involve them in thinking about their classroom goals and structure. While the binder isn't just for math, it can contain a page titled "How We Work During Math Class." Working on this page with the students can help clarify your expectations. When visitors come, a student host can introduce the binder to them as a way of helping acquaint them with the class.

## 13 What kinds of questions best support math learning?

Questions are vital for supporting math learning. They invite students to think mathematically, connect what they already know to what they're currently studying, formulate and communicate new ideas, justify procedures, and defend the reasonableness of their answers. Also, students' responses to questions give you information that helps you assess what they know. Students need to understand these two purposes of questions: to help them learn and to help you know what they understand.

With these broad purposes in mind, we think about questions in several categories. One category includes questions that call for one correct answer, such as when you ask children how much is 4 plus 3, 15 plus 23, or the sum of any two numbers. Questions that have a right answer are most effective for promoting mathematical thinking when they have answers a child can figure out, not when they call for some memorized bit of information. There are times, of course, when you ask a question that requires a memorized answer, for example, "What do we call the number on the top of a fraction?" But keep in mind that questions like these focus on mathematical conventions, not mathematical reasoning. The bulk of classroom questions should foster thinking.

Another category of questions are those that call for more than one correct answer. For example, instead of asking for sums as above, ask for two numbers that add up to 7 or 38. There's more than one correct answer to these questions, offering the opportunity for more children to respond. While these questions still focus on addition, they also support thinking about relationships among numbers.

Another category of questions focuses on asking children to explain theories or make conjectures. They may have one correct answer or more than one correct answer, but these questions probe more deeply. Here are examples of questions that fit in this category:

How many different pairs of addends are there that add to 7? to 38? to any number?

How can you tell without dividing if a number is divisible by 6? by 20?

Why can't a triangle have more than one right angle?

How might you change the rules of a game so that it's fair for both players?

Included in this category are questions that ask students to apply what they've learned in new situations. For example, try asking "What if?" questions, changing one or more conditions of an original problem or situation:

What if we rolled three dice? What sum will most likely come up more often than others?

What if we wanted to find three numbers that add up to 7?

What if we add two even numbers? Will the answer be even or odd? What if we add two odd numbers or one even and one odd number? What if we multiply?

Avoid questions that can be answered merely by "yes" or "no," because these can close down instead of open up discussion. For example, instead of asking, "Do you understand what _____ said?" ask, "Can you explain why _____'s idea does (or doesn't) make sense?" At every opportunity, questioning should contribute to the development of students' mathematical reasoning. We know that students have caught on to the importance of questions like this when we hear them asking similar questions of one another, often in the same tone of voice we use!

## 14 I know it's important for students to understand what they're learning. But sometimes I just want to tell them how to do something. Is this all right?

The nature of what you're teaching is the key to deciding when it's appropriate to tell students something and when telling won't serve their learning. What's important here is whether the source of the knowledge for the child is external or internal. We'll try to explain.

Some knowledge is based solely on social convention or customs and, therefore, is accessible only from sources outside the child. For example, there isn't a logical reason that we celebrate Thanksgiving on a Thursday in November each year; it's an arbitrary social custom. So is setting a table with forks on the left of the plate and knives and spoons on the right. There isn't any way to figure out or discover this sort of information by relying only on your internal resources. You have to hear the information, read about it in a book, see it on television, or learn it from some other means. From repeated use, you memorize this kind of information and draw upon it when you need it. If you forget it, you'd have to check with someone else or look it up again; you couldn't figure it out.

In mathematics, we use many social conventions that children have to learn. The plus sign, for example, and the symbols for subtraction, multiplication, and division are all arbitrary conventions. Also, we use commas to separate digits in large numbers and a period to indicate that what follows is a decimal. In England, however, it's the reverse; a comma indicates a decimal numeral and periods are used to separate digits in large numbers! Therefore, teaching by telling is appropriate for helping children learn conventional symbols; you're imparting knowledge that is social in nature and for which the source of the knowledge is outside the learner.

Learning most of mathematics, however, relies on understanding its logical structures. The source of logical understanding is internal, requiring a child to process information, make sense of it, and figure out how to apply it. Hearing and then memorizing doesn't develop understanding. While a child can be told how to read a large number—32,475, for example—and told the names of the places—ones, tens, hundreds, thousands, and so on—understanding the place value system of our numbers requires that they learn its structure. We can explain the logic, but children have to make sense of it for themselves. To engage children in learning the logic of mathematical ideas, we involve them in activities that promote their thinking and reasoning. Working with problem-solving situations helps, using manipulative materials helps, and so does explaining ideas and considering the ideas of others. But the learning goes on inside each child's mind.

All of us have learned the procedure for dividing fractions and can probably get the correct answer to a division of fractions problem. Sadly, however, many of us can't really explain the logic of why we turn one fraction upside down and then multiply. It's as if we were taught: Yours is not to question why, just invert and multiply. The procedure works, but to teach it as if it were a social custom rather than a method steeped in basic principles of numerical understanding doesn't support building mathematical competence. It's a shortsighted decision.

So . . . this is a long-winded way to advise you to let the source of the knowledge you're trying to teach your students determine how you'll teach it. If it's social knowledge, telling is fine. If the knowledge calls for understanding a logical construct, then not only is telling a poor approach, but it leads to mathematical dead ends.

We believe this theory is sound. But we also know that in the thick of classroom instruction, even the most solid theory can be difficult to heed. Many of us, for example, have experienced a student saying to us, "I don't get it. If you'll just tell me what to do, I'll do it." This is usually when a student is more focused on finishing an assignment than on understanding. Or, worse yet, it's when a student thinks that something is just supposed to be memorized rather than to make sense. While the temptation in situations like these may be to relieve the tension by telling students what to do, it's important to remember the benefit of this decision is short-lived.

## 15 How can I assess my students to find out if they're learning what I'm teaching?

Assessment is an ongoing aspect of instruction, and it's useful to think about assessing your students in several ways. One is by listening to the responses they offer in whole-class lessons. Another is by walking around the classroom when students are working in small groups or individually, listening to what they are saying to one another or asking questions to probe their thinking. Both of these are informal opportunities that occur in conjunction with instruction. The information you gather, although seemingly incidental in nature, is valuable.

For example, many teachers use the day's date to help their children focus on writing equations for numbers. On the ninth day of the month, for example, the children think of number sentences that produce the number 9, and the teacher records their ideas on the board. For young children, this most often initially translates to thinking about addition combinations and later to subtraction problems as well. For older students, the teacher can make other requirements such as having to use each of the four operations at least once ($4 \times 6 \div 8 + 10 - 4 = 9$), having to use only four 4s and any combinations of operations ($4 \div 4 + 4 + 4 = 9$), or using the number 100 in the sentence ($100 - 81 = 9$). An activity like this is not only a good way to begin the day's math class, but it's also useful for listening to children's responses and learning about their numerical comfort and ability.

Instead of having a whole-class discussion to collect equations, however, children can work in pairs or small groups to brainstorm number sentences. In this case, circulate through the room and listen as students work. After a few minutes, call the class to attention. Then go around the room and give each group a chance to offer a number sentence for you to record on the board. Make the rule that a group must report a sentence that you haven't already written. Groups may pass if they have no new ideas, but continue until groups have offered all of their thoughts.

While observing in whole-class and small-group settings provides valuable information about students, it's also important for you to find out specifically what each student knows. Many children are talkative and willing to participate in class. Their hands shoot up in the air regularly to provide answers and explanations. But other children are reticent to volunteer in whole-class discussions, and some are also quiet in small groups. You need to have ways to collect information about these children's learning as well, and you can accomplish this through written assignments or one-on-one interviews.

For example, after listing half a dozen or so of the students' number sentences on the board, ask children to write five more equations on their own. You may want to give an extra challenge to this assignment. Here are some options for extensions:

Think of sentences with three or more numbers that add up to our date.

Write sentences that include at least one multiplication.

Write sentences that use only fractions or decimals, no whole numbers.

Their papers will reveal their capability to do the work; their choice of numbers can give you further information about their numerical comfort.

A one-on-one interview is probably the most valuable way to assess the depth of a child's thinking. Doing so with even a few of your students will not only give you access into those children's understanding but also help you think more deeply about the mathematics you're teaching.

## 16 I'd like to try some one-on-one interviews to assess my students. How can I do this during class time?

There's really no other way to assess a student's understanding that's comparable to conducting one-on-one interviews. Talking with individual children gives you a window into their thinking and reasoning that simply isn't available from students' written work or participation in whole-class discussions.

There are several aspects to preparing for one-on-one interviews—deciding what questions you'll ask, making time to hold an individual conversation, setting the stage with a student for a successful interview, and making use of the results. Of these, we find the first aspect, deciding on the questions to ask, to be the most critical. Think about sitting across a desk from one of your students. What do you want to know? What questions might you ask? What problems would be suitable to reveal the child's understanding and skills? Remember that your goal is to gain understanding of children's reasoning as well as what they can do.

For example, suppose you want to assess a second grader's numerical facility. You might start by asking the child to count out 20 beans or tiles. Cover them with a sheet of paper and then remove 6 or 7 of them. Show the child the beans or tiles you removed and ask how many are still under the paper. Does the child know instantly? If not, how does the child figure out the answer? Is the answer correct? Can the child explain how he or she reasoned? Remember that an answer without an explanation doesn't reveal how a child thinks. Don't rely on doing this just once. If a child answers incorrectly, try again with a number that's smaller than 20, perhaps 10. If a child answers correctly, pose another problem as a check. Also, you might ask the child to write down a math sentence or equation that describes this math problem.

With older students, you might be interested in their understanding of fractions. Pose a problem that calls for using fractions. It could be something they've done in class so you can see how they work on their own. For example, ask a student to share cookies fairly among a group of friends. Ask, "If there were 4 people and 3 cookies, how much would each get?" Be sure that the student knows that fair shares mean that each person gets the same amount of cookie. As with the younger children, ask the student to write a math equation to describe the problem and also to record the amount of cookie each person gets. Change the number of people and cookies for follow-up problems.

For both younger and older students, keep interviews fairly short. We find that five or ten minutes used well is enormously helpful to learn about a child. And a short interview makes it easier to figure out a time when you can conduct the assessment without being interrupted. It's difficult to do when you're in the midst of managing whole-class instruction. If it's important to have a one-on-one conversation with a particular student, arrange to do so when the other students are elsewhere, perhaps at the library. If an interview is short, it shouldn't pose a sacrifice to have a child miss a particular activity this one time, especially if the information you learn will help you meet that specific child's needs.

About setting the stage: We recommend that you tell the child why you're having the conversation, that you're interested in finding out as much as possible about what he or she does and doesn't yet know in math so that you can think about how to help him or her learn. Tell students the most important thing is that you understand how they think, that you can't peer into their eyes or peek into their ears and get a glimpse of how their brain works mathematically. The only way you can understand how their brain is working is to ask them to tell or show you. That's why you want them to talk out loud as much as possible and, at times, write things down.

You can make use of what you learn in individual interviews in two ways: to gain insights into the individual student's math progress and to inform and improve your overall classroom instruction. Think about the questions you asked that gave you specific information about the student, information that would help you, for example, in a conversation with the student's parents or with another colleague about the student's math progress. Then think how to integrate those questions into your classroom teaching.

We realize that it's difficult to arrange and manage individual assessments in light of the demands of a typical teaching day, and it's most likely not possible to arrange for one-on-one conversations with all students. But we urge you to pursue individual assessments with at least some of your students. We've found the benefits to be well worth the effort.

## 17 What should I do if I plan lessons that are too hard or too easy?

Without a doubt, your students will let you know if something you try with them is too difficult. The feedback may be in the form of a barrage of questions and comments relating to the assignment: "What do I do?" "I don't get it!" "Can you help me?" Or, the remarks may be less related to the lesson you've presented or the assignment you've given and appear to be a negative attitude: "This is boring." "I don't like this." "Do I have to do this?" Also, children's responses in a whole-class discussion or on their written work can let you know when they don't understand.

However you get the feedback, the best way to deal with it is to acknowledge it. Say to students, "I don't think what I planned is helping you learn. It seems like you're confused and frustrated, and I'm not feeling good about the lesson. What can you tell me about the problem?" Then listen. Accept what they say without being defensive. As students verbalize what they don't understand, try to ascertain whether they have all of the skills needed to acquire understanding. For example, young students facing the addition of numbers in the teens may not yet be comfortable enough with number combinations for 10. Students have difficulty estimating the product of two- and three-digit numbers if they don't understand the patterns of multiplying by 10, 100, and 1,000. Remind students that it's your job to help them learn. Make sure you explain that the math ideas are important for them to know, and that you'll try another approach that might be less confusing and more successful. Your new approach may involve a more concrete, hands-on experience or a way for them to review previously presented material. In any case, your children need to know that you think they're capable of learning the material and that you'll take responsibility for presenting it in a way that they can be successful.

You'll also be able to sense if something you present is too easy. Sometimes students will whip through an assignment in much less time than you anticipate. Most often, however, an assignment is too easy for only a handful of students who may remark, "We did this last year." When you plan lessons, have extensions in mind for these students. The purpose of the extensions isn't to load them down with more work, but to extend the lesson—to challenge them with a thinking activity that will engage them. (*See page 28 for ideas about extensions.*) When introducing an extension to children, you might say, "I notice that the work I've assigned is really easy for you. That's terrific. But what's important in math is that you can think about something you know in different ways. Here's something I'd like you to try. I'm interested in seeing how you make sense of it. And I'm interested in your opinion about whether you think other students would benefit from this new challenge."

It's not unusual for some students to find the work too hard or too easy. The best preparation for dealing with these situations is to know whether students possess the prerequisite learning for the lesson as well as how to extend the mathematics. Your intent should be on giving children the opportunity to work to the edges of their own ability boundaries.

### 18 I've heard that when assigning a problem, first you should have volunteers discuss how they might go about figuring it out. Doesn't this give too much away for the others?

It helps to make a distinction between a learning activity and a testing situation. When you are testing each child's ability to solve a particular kind of problem or demonstrate a particular skill, then it makes sense to ask the children to work independently in order to show what they can do. But the bulk of the children's math time should focus on their learning, which means providing them the most help you can in order for them to understand something new or build new learning on top of what they already know. A class discussion helps make different approaches and ideas accessible to others. It can help a child who was perplexed know how to begin. It can offer alternative approaches to students who already had a particular idea. In either case, nothing is lost, and increased learning can result.

Sometimes in an initial discussion, a volunteer blurts out an answer. When this happens, reinforce that you're interested both in the answer and the thinking they did to figure it out. One way to respond is, "I'm not interested in just the answer at this time. I'm interested in your ideas about how you might go about finding the answer or checking that an answer you have is correct."

Then ask each child to record a solution and explain how he or she reached it. It's fine for students to use an idea suggested by a classmate, but they should explain it in their own words. Keep the learning focus clear: *Do only what makes sense to you.* Also, make a practice of asking students to think about at least two different ways to figure out an answer. This encourages students to try out others' ideas and become flexible in their mathematical thinking.

### 19 What about cooperative groups in math class—do they really help?

We think that having students work cooperatively is extremely helpful. In order to make sense of the math they're learning, students need as many opportunities as possible to talk about what they're thinking and how they're reasoning. Cooperative groups can make that happen. When working in groups, students talk about their ideas and learn from others' thinking, which helps them develop, cement, and extend their understanding.

Of course, merely putting students in groups doesn't guarantee learning. First of all, you'll need to work with students so that they have clear guidelines for being a productive member of a cooperative group, whether it be a pair of children or a group of three, four, or five students. An important expectation is that all of the students in a group participate and understand what the group is doing. Also, you should be able to question any group member at any time and get a report on the group's progress.

There are different ways that groups can work. At times they'll work together, collaborating on an investigation or solving a particular problem. One useful rule of thumb when you want the group to work closely together is to let the students know that you'll offer your assistance when everyone in the group has the same question, and only then. This helps avoid a situation in which one child has a question and seeks your help before talking with the others in the group. At other times, students will be doing individual work, but their group members will be available to support, willing to help when asked. And at still other times, you'll want students to work individually without help from classmates. This is essential for finding out what individual students know. In these cases, give the children guidelines about what you expect. When students are given clear information about how you want them to work and why, they're more apt to understand what you want and be willing to conform.

Teachers have different systems for putting children into groups. Some have children sit in groups all of the time so that it's easy for them to work together when directed to do so. While some of these teachers leave the groups more or less the same for the year, others change the seatings on a regular basis, such as every month. Many teachers place students into groups randomly; one method is to distribute playing cards and have the aces, twos, threes, and so on sit together, using two, three, or four of each number card, depending on the size groups you're forming. Other teachers prefer to assign partners or groups. Whatever the system, both the mechanics and the rationale for your particular method should be clear to the students. For example, a reason for grouping children randomly might be because you feel it's important that they have the opportunity to work with all of their classmates during the year. Or you might assign partners or groups because of children's particular interests.

When first introducing students to working cooperatively, it's important to choose math activities that foster cooperation. Be sure the task is appropriate for all students, choose a task that's accessible to those with less ability while also offering a challenge to students with more aptitude and interest. For example, second graders worked in pairs and compared the first letters of their names. Together they wrote two lists, one describing how the letters were alike, for example, both have only straight lines, and the other describing how they were different, for example, one makes a fence that would keep the dog in and the other doesn't. Fourth graders worked in groups of four to find all the different shape rectangles they could make with color tiles for all the numbers from 1 to 25. (*See Figure 2–1.*)

When groups are working, circulate and listen. This is an effective way to learn about how children are thinking. Join groups that seem to be stuck and offer help as needed and probe thinking when you see the opportunity. Have a class discussion afterward so that groups can hear about how other groups worked and what they discovered.

### 20 How can I decide whether the best approach for a lesson is for students to work individually, with partners, in small groups, or as a whole class?

Following are some simple guidelines for deciding which organization is most appropriate in a situation. If you're giving the students information that you want everyone to know about, or if one of the students is offering ideas that are valuable for the entire class to hear, then whole-class instruction makes best sense. There's no point in putting children in groups and then going around to deliver the same information to each group. It's more efficient for all of them to hear information at the same time, and this guarantees that they all receive the same version of the message.

But even when students receive the same message, they don't necessarily hear it in the same way. To process information, it helps students to have a chance to talk about it. In whole-class discussions, only one person talks at a time. In small groups, however, more of the students can talk at the same time and, therefore, more have the chance to be actively involved at the same time. This more widespread involvement is also useful when you want students to engage in an investigation or solve a problem.

However, when you want to know about what individual students understand and can do, then individual work makes best sense. At these times, ask students

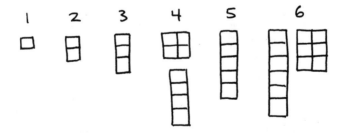

**2–1.** Students use color tiles to build all the possible shape rectangles for different numbers.

not to talk to one another but to do their best to show you what they do and don't understand.

It's good to vary the classroom structure to involve students in all three types of situations; a variety makes instruction more engaging for the students. Also, for some lessons, you'll want a mix of groupings. For example, you might begin in a whole-class setting. You might ask second graders to estimate the number of cubes in a jar and then, as the whole class watches, empty the jar one by one and count to determine that there are 32 cubes. Then pose a problem: *If we put the cubes into groups of five each, how many groups will there be?* Have students discuss the problem in groups or with a partner. After a few minutes, call the class back to attention and discuss their ideas. Then actually put the cubes into groups of five, count the groups, and then count the cubes by 5s—5, 10, 15, 20, 25, 30, and two more makes 32. Repeat, this time asking groups to figure out how many groups there would be if you put the cubes into groups of two each. Then rearrange the cubes, count the groups, and count the cubes by 2s—2, 4, 6, 8, 10, and so on. Finally, for an individual assignment, ask students to figure out how many groups there would be if you grouped the cubes into 10s.

## 21 After I give my class directions for an activity, it seems that there's a flurry of hands from students who want assistance. What can I do about this?

No matter how clear you think your directions are, it always seems that some students are confused and not sure what to do. This problem exists in all subject areas, not just mathematics. We have three suggestions.

One is to have students describe what to do before you set your class loose on any assignment. Ask, "Who can give the directions in your own words?" or, "Who can say aloud what you're supposed to do now?" Urge the others to listen and be sure that they agree. Have at least two students offer their versions. After each, ask if anyone has something to change or add.

Another idea, when suitable for the particular assignment you give, is to tell students to check with a partner or the others at their table first before raising a hand. If this doesn't help, then both students or all members of a group should raise a hand to signal to you that they all have some confusion.

One more suggestion is to bring a kitchen timer to school. After giving directions and having some students repeat them, tell the class that you're setting the time for five minutes and that they need to work on their own at least until they hear the "bing." Then, if they haven't resolved their problem, you'll be happy to come and help. This system can encourage students to be more independent and self-reliant.

## 22 Some students always finish assignments quickly. What should I have them do?

This is a typical situation in class, and the best way to prepare is to anticipate it. Have an option ready for those students who learn and work more quickly. Try to make the option an extension that relates to the work at hand but offers a further challenge. When possible, offer an option that the students who finished first can work on together.

A caution: When situations like these occur, it doesn't seem right merely to assign additional similar problems to students who finish quickly. Most likely, they're the students who understand best and probably don't need more practice. That's why the extra work you give them should challenge them to extend their knowledge. (Of course, this isn't always the case, so be sure to take a careful look at papers to see if a student's work needs correction or improvement.)

For example, second graders were shown two containers, each with some cubes in it. They couldn't see how many cubes were in each, but they were told how many cubes there were in the two containers altogether. When they were first introduced to the activity, fewer than 10 cubes were used, and the children learned to record addition combinations for the possibilities. Next, as an individual assignment, they were to figure out how many cubes could possibly be in each container when there were 15 cubes in all. (*See Figure 2–2.*)

As usual, Andrew finished first and brought up his paper. A talented math student, he had approached the problem in an orderly way and was sure he had found them all. He had. Becky, Mario, and Celia also finished quickly. They didn't approach the problem in the orderly way Andrew did, but they had found most of the possibilities and felt they were done. The others were still working. The children who finished more quickly were given the challenge of figuring out the combinations for the 15 cubes if there were three containers instead of two.

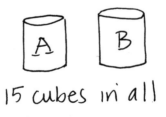

**2–2.** What are the possible combinations of cubes that could be in the two containers?

Older students were given a similar sort of problem. Their assignment was to figure out how many red, blue, and yellow cubes might be in a container, using a set of three clues.

Clue 1: *There are fewer than 25 cubes.*

Clue 2: *Two colors have the same number of cubes.*

Clue 3: *There are twice as many blue cubes as red cubes.*

The problem had multiple solutions, and their task was to find as many of them as they could. Katia quickly found four solutions; Peter and Jaime each found six; Hattie found eight; the rest of the students were continuing to work. As an extension, students who finished first were asked to write a fourth clue that would narrow the possibilities to one correct solution.

For some assignments, it's possible to ask students who finish quickly to sit in a small group, compare their papers, and see if they all agree. If there are differences, they should try to figure out why. When they all agree, they should revise their papers and let you know. This strategy worked in both situations above. But it won't always be appropriate. Sometimes the assignment doesn't lend itself to this sort of collaboration, or you may prefer that the students tackle an extension individually.

As an organizational issue, it helps to decide ahead of time whether it's best to have written directions for the extension, if you'd prefer to explain it to children as they complete their work, or if you plan to explain it to one child who will then tell the others. Thinking through details like these will help any lesson go more smoothly.

## 23   I spend an hour planning a classroom activity or assignment that takes my students five minutes to complete. How can I fix this picture?

Keep in mind the "input/output" rule: A teacher's input time for planning and preparing a lesson should be less than the students' output time. This means that it should take you less time to get ready for a lesson—thinking about the mathematics, planning the instruction, gathering the materials, and preparing an assignment and extensions—than the class time required for students to engage with the lesson, by trying an activity, having a discussion, working in small groups, and completing an assignment.

We know that planning and preparing are time-consuming, especially when content is complex and perhaps new to you. Have you heard the saying that you always know something best when you've taught it? That's because teaching calls for analyzing content and then making plans for how to present it logically and effectively to students. When you analyze and plan, you think about the ideas, turn them around, look at them from different perspectives, and consider alternatives for learning activities. In fact, you engage with all of the kinds of mental activities that are essential for really learning something new—the very mental activities that you'd like your students to experience.

Be careful not to synthesize your preparation time into a tidy and tight presentation. Learning is a process that's generally more messy than orderly and calls for trying out ideas, following leads, and revising thinking. For this reason, your students need at least the same amount of time to engage with the ideas and explore them as you did in preparation. And then, of course, they need time to practice, cement, and extend their understanding. In your lessons, don't rush for closure by the end of each math period; let lessons extend beyond a day's experience when needed. Push for depthful involvement and allow the time for it.

### 24 It seems important to be organized and have all the details of a lesson planned beforehand, but I feel that I'm doing too much planning. How can I change this?

Let's look at an example. Suppose you want your students to operate a make-believe store in order to practice dealing with money. To prepare, you might first select a variety of classroom items to "sell." Then you might decide how much each item should cost, write the prices on stickers or index cards, and attach them to the items. You might sort the items and figure out how best to set them out. If you want each child to have the same amount of money, you could count out the same collection of coins for each student in individual zip-top plastic baggies. Whew! The idea of applying money concepts to running a store is terrific, but you would need to spend hours just to get it ready.

Think. How can you plan this experience so that the children do the bulk of the work as well as the bulk of the learning? While the practice with money will be a valuable experience for the students, other learning can occur if you think differently about organizing the activity. First discuss with children what makes a store successful. Ask them to think about items that a classroom store should sell. Perhaps they might take some opinion polls and get involved in collecting, graphing, and interpreting data about their classmates' preferences. Once items are identified, engage the class in a discussion about how they might be sorted into "departments" in their store. Have the children write prices on stickers or index cards to label each item, which gives them practice representing money correctly. Give each child the same amount of spending money, but give it to them in the greatest denomination that they are familiar with so they will have to engage immediately in making change.

In the first scenario, you do all of the problem solving needed to establish a store, limiting the children's learning to their work with money. By having children identify, price, and sort the items before they buy or sell them, you give students the chance to apply an assortment of skills. But more importantly, they are actively involved in the planning and execution of the lesson. Because they are constructing it, they have ownership, an important ingredient for motivating their participation.

# Three | Leading Class Discussions

*Marc felt great about the how the math lesson was going. His students were engaged in the activities he prepared. They were using the manipulatives responsibly and productively, and they were recording their results carefully. There was a nice hum in the room.*

*But there was still a nagging feeling in the pit of Marc's stomach. He planned to pull the children together to discuss what they had done and discovered, but whenever he did so for math, the discussions seemed to fall flat. There were always a few kids who waved their hands, eager to participate, but others appeared listless, sometimes inattentive, and not very interested in communicating. Sometimes when he called on children, they just shrugged or claimed that they couldn't explain their thinking. Also, when students offered erroneous ideas or incorrect answers, Marc wasn't sure how to respond to keep them involved and learning. He didn't want to call on the same students all of the time, but he seemed to resort to this solution. Marc felt that class discussions were important for the students' learning, and he wanted help in improving them.*

## 25 How do I establish a classroom atmosphere that encourages students to participate in class discussions?

Responding in front of the entire class is risky, more for some students than for others. It's essential that you create a classroom atmosphere that is accepting and encouraging and promotes risk taking. This calls for maintaining a spirit in the classroom that is exploratory, lighthearted, and supportive. Listen to students attentively and give them ample time to complete their thoughts. Be curious about how they think. Expect students to listen respectfully to their classmates. Emphasize to the class that correct answers are important in mathematics but are only useful if students can justify that they make sense and also figure out similar problems.

Give students "think time" before you call on someone to respond. Thought takes time and you want children to think before blurting out answers or ideas. One way is to silently count slowly to ten before calling on anyone. As you wait, students come to realize that you're giving them time to think.

Another idea is to tell your students, "In our class, it's okay for you to change your mind at any time." Learning means coming to new understandings and that often calls for giving up erroneous notions. But also add, "If you change your mind, you also need to be able to explain why." This keeps the focus on their thinking, not on whim or social pressure.

It's helpful to talk with students about making errors. Minimize the risk of making mistakes by pointing out that all of us make errors and that errors are often the best opportunities for learning. When students make mistakes, encourage them to persist in their thinking and try to work through the challenge. Remind students often that it's important to understand whether an answer makes sense and why. As they gain confidence in sharing their answers and reasoning, children feel mathematically secure. And as they learn to feel more secure, they'll be more willing to take on challenges.

## 26   Are there general guidelines that can help me lead better math discussions?

This question first made us think about class discussions in general and why they're important. Class discussions are opportunities for students to share their knowledge, raise questions, try out new ideas, get feedback on their thinking—from classmates as well as from the teacher—and hear other points of view. They're useful whenever the issue to discuss is of value to all students. This can occur when you're introducing something new, clarifying something in the midst of an activity, or summarizing at the end of a lesson.

Class discussions not only support children's learning but are also valuable for us as teachers to assess our instruction. They can give us a general sense of the class's response to a particular lesson—how it was received and what students understand. Discussions don't replace the need for assessing individuals, of course, but they provide useful information.

To focus on children's thinking and push for understanding, we recommend the following general questions that we've found to be useful for prompting discussion:

**How did you figure out your answer?**

It's important for children to explain their reasoning every time they give an answer to a problem. Children's explanations are important windows into their thinking processes and give insights that answers alone don't provide. After you regularly ask students to explain their reasoning for a while, they will learn to include explanations with their responses without being prompted.

**How do you know your answer is reasonable?**

This helps children revisit a problem and reconsider their solution. Judging reasonableness helps students their build math sense.

**Who can explain what _____ said in your own words?**

Asking students to explain a classmate's idea is useful for cementing understanding. It also reminds children that there are different ways to express ideas.

**Who has another way to solve the problem (or approach the activity)?**

This reinforces that there are different ways to approach problems and activities and promotes flexibility in thinking. Sometimes a child's response will be similar to a previous one but will use different words. This is fine. It's beneficial for as many children as possible to have the chance to explain their ideas.

About logistics: Discussions are effective when everyone listens to the one person who is speaking. Be firm about your expectations about this for students. If sideline chatter is going on, stop the discussion and insist on attention to the speaker. There are times, however, when a comment sparks a spontaneous reaction and several students break into chatter. Remember that talking is useful for interpreting an idea and making sense of it. At times like this, it may be best to allow students a few moments to talk among themselves and voice their opinions in small groups. This way, more students get a chance to speak their mind. You can then call the class back to attention and have students report their ideas. *(For suggestions about encouraging reluctant students to participate in discussions, see page 40–41.)*

## 27 What's a good way to introduce discussion guidelines to my class?

The best way to introduce and implement discussion guidelines is in the context of class discussions. Give your students firsthand experience that puts the guidelines in action. For example, a teacher gathered her class near the chalkboard for a "math talk" discussion. She put three scoops of beans into a jar and asked the children to estimate the number of scoops it would take to fill the jar to the top. Many hands shot up. The teacher was interested in hearing how students would use the information that the jar was now about one-third full to make their estimates. But when called on, students typically just reported a number. After each estimate, however, she asked, "Can you tell us why you think that's a good estimate?" After repeating this request for several students, she shortened the question and merely prompted, "Because?" Finally, students caught on and began to offer explanations without additional encouragement.

The teacher then told the children that she was going to empty the jar, use the same scoop, and fill it a second time, but this time with scoops of rice. She asked the class, "Do you think there will be more scoops, fewer scoops, or the same number of scoops of rice as beans?" A flurry of conversation broke out, but the teacher quieted the class and told the students that she wanted them to talk one at a time so that they could hear one another's ideas. She reminded them to raise a hand to let her know that they wanted to contribute. Before she called on a child to respond, she gave another reminder, "When someone is talking, listen carefully to see if you agree or if your idea is different."

She called on Sarah first, asked the others to lower their hands, and waited until they did so before signaling Sarah to speak. Sarah then said, "I think there will be more scoops of rice." Other hands then shot up. The teacher asked them to lower their hands again. "Sarah hasn't finished yet," she said, "because she needs to tell us why she thinks there will be more scoops of rice than beans." Sarah looked a bit caught off guard at the teacher's comment; she still wasn't used to explaining her answers. She thought for a moment and said, "Because the rice is smaller." "Do you have anything more to add?" the teacher asked. When Sarah declined, the teacher addressed the class. "Who agrees with Sarah that there will be more scoops of rice?" Hands shot up. She waited a moment and asked, "Who has a reason that's different from the reason Sarah gave?" In this way, she reinforced that children were to pay attention when their classmates offered ideas. Often in classroom discussions, students merely wait for a classmate to stop talking so they can have their own turn. However, communication works best when students listen and respond to one another.

The discussion continued until all students who wanted had a chance to communicate their thinking. The children's different points of view contributed to a lively discussion. The teacher then had them return to their desks to write about how many scoops of rice they thought would fill the jar and why. She wrote a prompt on the board: I think that _____ scoops of rice will fill the jar because _____.

This particular lesson was done with third graders, but it works well in other grades as well. It's a good example for showing how to make discussion guidelines explicit in the context of an actual lesson. It's also a good lesson for this purpose because it engages students' curiosity and doesn't require complex thinking that would exclude anyone. Finally, don't forget to scoop the rice to prove that a scoop is a scoop, that a nine-scoop jar will hold nine scoops of either beans or rice!

After the class has had several experiences with whole-class discussions, you might post guidelines as a reference. For example:

Share your ideas.

Explain your reasoning.

Listen when someone is speaking.

Hands down when someone is speaking.

Comment on others' ideas.

## 28 My students ask me why they have to explain their thinking all the time. How should I answer this?

The social interaction of communicating ideas is one of the essential ingredients for learning. For too long, math was seen as a subject done in isolation. Many of us remember our own elementary school experience of doing seat work in math class. Our teachers directed us to keep our papers covered, and we'd use a protective gesture so students sitting nearby couldn't see what we were writing. Helping was often considered cheating. Times have changed!

It's important to reinforce for students that when you ask them to talk—and write—about their mathematical ideas, they have to organize and clarify their mathematical thinking, express their thoughts, and explain their reasoning. Point out how communicating gives them opportunities to use correct mathematical terminology. Emphasize that they benefit not only from talking and writing but also from listening to and considering the ideas and strategies offered by others.

Then follow up by making consistent use of prompts such as those in the following list. These should be standards in your teaching repertoire. The more you use them, the more quickly students will learn that you expect them to include their reasoning as part of answers and consider the ideas of others.

Explain how you figured.

What do you think?

Why do you think that?

Tell some more about what you're thinking.

Who has another way to explain that?

Why do you agree or disagree with _____'s answer?

Can you find another way to explain that?

## 29 Sometimes when I ask children to explain their thinking, they say, "I just know." Then what should I do?

This is a common occurrence in classrooms, especially when students haven't had much experience with verbalizing how they reason. With practice, however, they will improve. To help them improve, the best thing you can do is prompt, probe, and push—whatever it takes to jump-start their explanations. There's no foolproof way to do this, but try some of these questions: "What was the first thing you thought about? Where did you go from there? Could you draw a picture to show us what you did? How would you tell someone who was absent (or who is in a younger grade) what you were thinking?"

If a student is still unable to offer an explanation, you might try asking if someone else in the class could try to explain. This can model for the student what sort of explanation you're asking for and help a student look at his or her own thinking. Then ask the student if the classmate's explanation was similar to the way he or she was thinking and, if not, can he or she explain why.

To help students learn to explain their thinking, provide time for them to talk in small groups. This gives more students the chance to talk at the same time, and small groups are often less threatening settings for students to share their ideas in. Then individual students can report for their groups.

## 30 I'm nervous that I won't be able to understand children when they're explaining their ideas. What tips can you give me?

First of all, when planning a lesson, think about the mathematical ideas underlying the lesson and plan how to pose questions that can push students to think about those ideas. Then try to anticipate how students might respond to your questions. Finally, consider what might be appropriate responses to student comments that would keep the focus of the lesson on your goal. We realize that this is hard to do when you're teaching something for the first time, but it's a useful exercise for being as prepared as possible.

When you don't understand a student's response, honestly say so. You might say, "Can you explain that again? I need a little more help to understand your idea." Or, "Tell me more about what you're thinking." Or, "Can someone else explain this in a different way to help me understand?" Doing this not only can help you figure out what's on a child's mind but also models that you value persistence in understanding others' ideas.

We have one caution to offer when listening to students: Sometimes we make the error as teachers of listening for the answer we expect or would like to hear. This can result in not understanding what a child is saying or misinterpreting a child's response. Instead, we should put our attention to listening intently to what students say and trying to understand their thinking. For example, when asking students to explain how to tell if a number is even or odd, you may be hoping for a specific answer. Perhaps you are hoping for an explanation about looking at the final digit, that if a number ends in 0, 2, 4, 6, or 8, then it's even, and that otherwise, it's odd. However, a child might offer a completely different idea. There are several ways to explain why a number is even or odd: If you divide a number by 2 and the remainder is 0, then it's even; if the remainder is 1, then it's odd. Or, if you can represent the number as the sum of two identical addends, as long as both addends are whole numbers, then a number is even; if you can't, it's odd. Or, if you can represent a number as 2 times another whole number, then it's even; if not, it's odd.

Suppose a child answered, "If you can split it in two parts, it's even." The child may understand what even numbers are, but the answer isn't quite precise. It doesn't stipulate that the two parts would be the same. (One response that would offer the student a contradiction is, "I can 'split' 7 into 4 and 3, but I know that 7 isn't even.") Nor does the child's answer stipulate that the two parts must be whole numbers. (Another response you might offer is, "I can 'split' 7 equally into $3\frac{1}{2}$ and $3\frac{1}{2}$, but 7 still isn't even.") Acknowledge the student's thinking and push for more. Say something like, "I think your answer is a good start, but it needs to be more complete." Then ask the student if he or she would like to try again or get help from a classmate.

### 31 Can't class discussions be too confusing for some students? I've seen struggling students who barely grasp one strategy and just fog out when others give their ideas.

As much as we all hate to admit it, it's more than likely that some students will tune out in a class discussion, either because they don't understand or they're not interested. Also, we know that it's often difficult to follow someone else's reasoning; as teachers, we've all experienced blank reactions from students after we thought that we gave an extremely clear explanation about why something makes sense. While it may seem that these realities point to recommending we diminish the amount of time spent on class discussions in which students explain their reasoning, the opposite is actually true.

We've long been told that you know something best when you teach it. To prepare for teaching, you think about the material at hand and make sense of it for yourself. Turning ideas around in your head and making them your own enables you to offer them to others. Your active mental involvement is how you construct your own understanding. In the same way, we want students as often as possible to have opportunities to think through ideas for themselves, explain their thinking, and communicate with others. This sort of interaction is essential for students to construct their own understanding.

We know that students won't always understand what others say or always follow one another's reasoning. It's even tough for us at times to be sure that we're correctly understanding what a student is saying. But an important support for learning is to establish a classroom culture that encourages sharing of ideas and expects students to listen to and try to understand one another's ideas. Students need to know that they can learn from one another as well as from the teacher and from books.

## 32 I need help with responding to students when they give wrong answers in a way that won't turn them off from math. What suggestions can you give me?

Teachers have told us they worry that telling students their answers are wrong will discourage them, stifle their thinking, and make them feel hopeless about math. We believe that correcting a child who has made an error can be helpful, not harmful. Besides, the potential danger of not pointing out errors is that students will believe their erroneous thinking was valid.

We have three suggestions to guide you when a student comes up with a wrong answer: be honest, be supportive, be helpful. A model that may be helpful to think about is one of individual lessons, perhaps for playing a musical instrument or learning a sport. When you make an error in that situation, the teacher will point it out and give you feedback and typically will either give you a chance to try again right then or some suggestions for more practice. This doesn't turn a student off, because the student has a goal to achieve—either to play a particular musical piece or be better at playing a game. The teacher and the student actually have the same goal: the student's success. They both know that understanding, rigor, and practice are essential.

While learning math isn't exactly the same as learning to play an instrument or a sport, we can improve our classroom teaching by thinking about instruction in those areas. The goal for math instruction should be clear: for students to think and reason mathematically and develop the skills they need to solve problems. The classroom atmosphere should be one in which risk taking is comfortable so that students will offer their thinking even if they're not sure it's right. And the feedback should help students build their understanding and refine their skills. Mistakes are a natural part of learning in every area and should be viewed not as colossal disasters, but as opportunities to investigate thinking.

It may seem less threatening to correct students in a one-to-one situation, such as a music lesson, where a child's privacy is protected. But we don't have that situation in classroom instruction. During a class discussion, try one of the following approaches when a student offers an erroneous idea.

The best way we know is to point out a contradiction to the student's thinking. For example, a student might incorrectly combine two fractions, $\frac{1}{2}$ and $\frac{1}{3}$, and get the wrong answer of $\frac{2}{5}$. To offer a contradiction, you might say, "When you add something to $\frac{1}{2}$, the sum ought to be larger. But your answer of $\frac{2}{5}$ is less than $\frac{1}{2}$. This doesn't make sense." Or a student might say, "A square is a four-sided shape with all sides the same length." In this case, you might give a visual contradiction by drawing a rhombus on the board and pointing out that it has four sides the same length but it's not a square. When offering a contradiction, be sure to do so with a wondering tone rather than a challenging one. Then give the student a chance to revise the answer.

We realize, however, that giving specific mathematical feedback by pointing out a contradiction isn't always possible. So we have several other responses that we've found to be helpful:

Give the student a chance to think again. Say, "Your answer doesn't make sense to me. Can you explain again?" Often students will self-correct when given a second chance.

Offer the student a choice about what to do next. Say, "When I did the problem, I got a different answer. Do you want to try again or listen to someone else's idea?"

Acknowledge that the answer is correct for a different problem. Say, "Your answer of 66 would be correct if I asked you to double 33, but the problem was to double 38." Then give the student the choice of either trying again or listening to someone else.

## 33   How can I keep from calling on the same students all of the time? In class discussions, it always seems to be the same students who raise their hands to answer.

This seems to be the case in most classes. A handful of students are always waving their hands, eager to answer, some students volunteer from time to time, and others seem never to be willing to contribute. This problem isn't particular only to math class, and our suggestions may help with other curriculum areas as well.

While the enthusiasm of students who are always willing to contribute is heartening, there are dangers if you call on them all of the time. Other students may feel excluded, worse yet unworthy, and worst of all may get into the habit of avoiding thinking and depending on those who generally monopolize class discussions. One more danger: the teacher may think that the entire class has the same knowledge as the quicker, more verbal students. This isn't necessarily so. Hearing critical information and other points of view can support others' learning, of course, but it's no guarantee. All students need the experience of talking in order to cement or extend their learning. Talking is like teaching; the more chances you have to verbalize and clarify your thinking, the deeper your understanding. Also, hearing from your students in discussions gives you a general vehicle for assessing students' responses to your lessons.

We have several suggestions for working to engage all students in class discussions. First, talk with your students about the importance of class discussions. Here are some ways you might phrase the value of class discussions. Tell your students:

Discussions give you the chance to try out ideas, which helps you learn.

Discussions allow you to hear the ideas of others, which can help you think about something in a new way.

Sharing ideas is part of learning how to work together as a class to help all students learn.

When I hear your ideas, it helps me think more about lessons I can prepare to help you learn.

Then let your students know that part of their responsibility as students is to contribute to class discussions. Acknowledge that it's harder for some people than others, but it's important for everyone to do so. There are few secrets in a class, and students know who loves to talk and for whom it's very difficult. Offer them ways to help one another. For example, having students talk in pairs or small groups before asking anyone to respond to the entire class can give reluctant students more confidence about speaking up. Also, be sure to allow enough wait time after asking a question for all students to think. As a regular practice, tell students that you want to hear from someone who hasn't yet contributed.

When one child is talking, keep your eyes on that child and listen carefully to what he or she is saying. Demand that the rest of the students do the same. If others are talking or seem to be distracted when a classmate is about to talk, stop the speaker and ask for everyone's attention. Also, ask the others to lower their hands. Raised hands can be distracting to the speaker and can also indicate that children are thinking about what they're going to say when it's their turn instead of listening to what's being said now.

Because talking in front of the class can be scary for students, make sure they know it's okay to make an error or not be completely right. We all learn from mistakes, and one student's error is an opportunity for everyone to benefit. Establishing a classroom environment that encourages the risk of offering even shaky ideas is essential. You can do this by modeling for your students how to be respectful and supportive and then expecting them to follow your lead with their classmates.

# Four | Number Sense and the Basics

*One of the report card grades that Stephanie had to enter was labeled "Number Sense," while another was labeled "Computation." "What do you consider to be number sense?" Stephanie asked her teammate, Cheryl. "How do you evaluate your children's number sense?"*

*Cheryl replied, "I'm a bit confused, too. I know that there are overlaps between the two. I think of computation as the basics, but does computation include the students knowing the times tables? They should have those memorized and not have to compute them, so maybe they're part of number sense."*

*Stephanie added, "And what about mental computation? It's computation, but number sense is a big part of figuring in your head."*

*"If this is confusing for us, imagine the kids' confusion!" Cheryl said. "We need some clarification."*

## 34 I hear a lot about students needing to know the "basics." What do the "basics" really include?

There are short answers and long answers to this question, and we offer some of them here to help you make sense of this issue.

The shortest answer is that "the basics" refers to arithmetic—one of the time-honored three Rs of elementary education.

Another short answer is that the basics are the "addition facts" and "multiplication facts." These generally refer to sums with addends from 1 to 10 and products with factors from 1 to 12. Having these committed to memory is one way of defining "knowing the basics."

Another short answer expands this view and defines the basics to include the ability to add, subtract, multiply, and divide with whole numbers, fractions, decimals, and percents—depending, of course, on the child's grade level. In this view, having the addition and multiplication tables committed to memory is important, but it's just one aspect of being able to compute with competence.

A slightly longer answer is that the basics include more than computational proficiency. Also basic to mathematical proficiency in this view, which is our view, is knowing how to apply computation skills. This includes being able to identify the operations that are appropriate in specific problem-solving situations; knowing how to evaluate the reasonableness of answers, which calls for being able to estimate; and successfully interpreting how answers relate to the problem at hand. To identify basic competency in mathematics merely as the ability to compute proficiently is as limited a view as thinking that a person who can play scales on an instrument is necessarily a competent musician.

We think that it's important for your students—and their parents—to think about basics in this expanded way. Arithmetic still is the major emphasis of elementary mathematics education. Committing the addition and multiplication tables to memory and learning to compute are important skills, but they are only part of the story. Applying computation skills to solve problems and developing good number sense are both essential ingredients of what's basic to children's math learning.

It may seem that we're being picky about the semantics of *basics*. But we don't think so. Our goal for math instruction is to define the basics as broadly as possible and not let a watered-down interpretation prevail. Children deserve better.

## 35 How can I help students memorize the addition and multiplication tables?

First of all, it's important that students see the usefulness of committing to memory the sums and products on the basic addition and multiplication tables. Ideally, students would learn these from using them over and over again in many different contexts, but even a rigorous regime of problem solving and performing mental calculations doesn't guarantee that students will memorize all of them. Some additional attention will most likely be needed.

One caution: Although students should understand why memorizing basics is important, a focus on memorization should follow *understanding*. Emphasize learning the facts after students have developed understanding of the concept, can perform computations (even if not efficiently), and have had a good deal of experience using the skills in problem-solving situations. Then it's time to take a check and see what students need to study in order to memorize. When should this happen? Districts have made different decisions about this, but we think it's reasonable to expect students to know the addition tables by the end of second grade and the multiplication tables by the end of fourth grade—meaning that children have quick and effortless recall of sums with addends from 1 to 10 and products with factors from 1 to 12.

When helping children learn, keep a focus on relationships among numbers. With young children, post an addition table and ask, "Which are the easy ones?" They'll identify the sums they already know. Children typically respond that it's easy to add 1 to a number, and you can cross out the sums in the column and row with 1 in them since they already know these. Children also often respond that they know the doubles. Typically, they know 2 + 2, 3 + 3, 4 + 4, 5 + 5—most likely because they can use their fingers—and 10 + 10. Cross these out. After eliminating the sums the students agree are easy, ask children to figure out one of the "harder" sums, perhaps 8 + 4. Talk with them about their strategies. Once you've established that 12 is the correct answer, tell the children that the answer to 8 + 4 also tells you the answer to 4 + 8. Ask children to explain why. The commutative property will be more immediately obvious to some children than others. Explain to the children, "Every number pair has a partner, and if you learn one sum, you've really learned two!" Ask the children to hunt for these pairs on the chart. They appear symmetrically on the diagonal, and children will be helped to see this pattern if you consistently cross them out on the same side of the diagonal. *(See Figure 4–1.)*

When you're done, there will be many fewer sums for the children to learn than the original one hundred. To help children with those that remain, lead discussions in which they share strategies for figuring. *(See page 46 for an example of doing this with 6 + 7.)*

To help older students focus on the multiplication table, involve them in brainstorming all of the possible ways they might memorize it. List their suggestions on

**4–1.** Eliminating simple combinations and reversed pairs makes the addition table easier to learn.

the board. Then have students choose one way that they'd like to try for memorizing a part of the table, say, the 8s. Children may opt to study alone or with a partner who chose the same method. They might choose some sort of written practice, oral practice, or some game or other available classroom aid. Identify a period of time, perhaps a week or two, and provide class time for study. At the end of that time, have students quiz one another. Keep two goals in mind: evaluating whether they've learned the facts and evaluating their choice of learning vehicle. Then repeat for another set of facts.

Also engage students in explorations that help them become more familiar with mathematical patterns in the table. For example, ask students if they think there are more even or odd products. Then have them check and discuss the answer. An investigation of products when factors are even or odd will contribute to their number sense while focusing on the times table. Or, ask students which product occurs most often on the multiplication table. Or, suggest that a student (erroneously) thought that $9 \times 7$ was the same as $8 \times 8$ since $9 + 7$ is the same as $8 + 8$. Ask the class to talk about why this works for addition but not for multiplication. Investigations such as these support students' learning.

## 36 Should I use timed tests?

Ah, this can be a controversial issue. We offer our reasons here about why we absolutely don't support timed tests, but we realize that there are different points of view. Our basic reason is that we make a distinction between *teaching* and *testing*. When we're teaching, we support learning in every way that we can. We like the environment to be supportive, risk-free, and filled with curiosity and exploration. These characteristics typically don't exist when we're testing. It makes sense to us that in order to learn, students need to be in teaching situations, not testing situations, and given all the assistance possible.

If you want to test your students' knowledge of addition and multiplication facts, then you should give a test. But don't fool yourself that a regular regimen of timed tests is a sensible way to teach. For those students who already know the tables, timed tests are a way to show their stuff. For those who don't, it can be a reoccurring defeating and humiliating experience. It's mean-spirited and unnecessary.

That's our view.

## 37 How much time should I devote to mental math?

Devote as much time to practice with mental math as you do for written computation practice. Computing mentally is a basic life skill that we use daily and deserves a fair share of math instructional time. Think about how you use arithmetic—calculating tips and dividing checks at restaurants, figuring when to leave home to arrive at the movies on time, doubling or halving recipes, keeping track of what you put in the supermarket cart so you don't go over the twenty dollars you have with you, and so on. More often than not when we do arithmetic, we don't reach for paper and pencil. We figure in our heads.

Engage your students often with mental math. Present classroom situations for them to solve, drawing on actual events whenever possible. Here are some problems that work with younger children:

Three children are absent today. How many students are here in class?

Let's figure out if everyone will have a partner when we line up for assembly.

Today 15 children bought milk for lunch. Did we collect more or less than $10?

Last week each child took out three books from the library. How many books will we return this week?

Here are some examples for older students:

About how much do you think our class spends on milk each week?

If we go to the movies on a field trip, how much will the admission cost?

The book we're reading now was written in 1979. How long ago was that?

The paperback book costs $12.95 in the bookstore. How much change would you get if you paid for it with a $20.00 bill?

Another reason for making mental math an integral part of your math program is that it builds children's number sense. Computing in your head calls for reasoning numerically and using methods appropriate for the numbers at hand, not necessarily following a standard procedure. Your students will benefit from hearing a variety of approaches and talking about different strategies for computing mentally. Second graders, for example, were asked to think about ways to add 6 plus 7. The students' ideas showed different levels of sophistication:

Start with 6 and count on 7.

Start with 7 and count on 6.

You know 6 plus 6 is 12, so one more is 13.

Take 4 from the 7 and put it on the 6 to make 10, then 3 more is 13.

Take 5 from the 6 and 5 from the 7 to make 10, then you have 1 and 2 left over, so the answer is 13.

For each suggestion, the teacher identified the general strategy the child used and listed it on a sheet of chart paper:

Count on.

Switch the numbers around and then count on. (The teacher chose this language instead of identifying the strategy as using the commutative property first)

Start with something you know.

Take numbers apart and put them together. (This strategy was used for the last two examples from the children, but the teacher listed it only once.)

The same instructional approach works for older students. Give them problems with larger numbers and other operations—doubling 76, 237, or other numbers, halving numbers, multiplying, dividing, and so on. Have students talk about their ideas and then help them generalize strategies.

### 38 I hear a lot about the importance of number sense. What exactly is number sense? How does it relate to basic facts?

It's tough to give an exact definition of number sense. Number sense is a broad idea that covers a range of numerical thinking skills. When children have good number sense, they think and reason flexibly with numbers, tend to make sound numerical judgments, and see numbers as useful. When children have poor number sense, they often don't notice when numbers are unreasonable, tend to follow procedures even when another way to reason is easier, and don't have good numerical intuition. We know two things for sure: number sense rests on making sense of mathematical concepts and procedures, and different people reason numerically in different ways. (Ask five friends to double 38 mentally and see the variety of methods they report.)

Basic facts are also a part of number sense. Calculations are easier when we know the basic facts. If our understanding is solid, we can always figure out answers to facts should we forget them, but knowing facts by heart contributes to efficiency and convenience. *(See page 43 for more about memorizing the basics.)*

### 39 Do you have any suggestions for assessing my students' number sense?

There isn't a simple checklist for assessing whether a student has strong number sense. But as you regularly offer numerical problem-solving experiences to the class, listen as students work together on a numerical problem, pay attention to their responses in class discussions, and assign written work that can give you further insights into how they reason. Observe students in action. For example, does the student

- show flexibility with numbers by drawing from several options when calculating, choosing methods that fit specific problems?
- show common sense and good intuition about numbers?
- have confidence and an "I can do it" attitude toward solving problems with numbers?
- make reasonable estimates in problem-solving situations?
- spot unreasonable answers?
- understand how numbers relate to one another and can be taken apart and put together in different ways? *(See page 46 for examples of how second graders used this skill.)*
- apply what he or she knows to new situations?

## 40 Can you really teach number sense?

Yes, you can teach number sense, and we have several suggestions. One is to link school math to real-world experiences. Present your class with problem situations that relate to their experiences, drawing on classroom routines whenever possible. *(See the mental math suggestions on page 46.)* Problems can also be derived from situations outside the classroom. For example, fifth graders were asked to compare two packages of raisins—a 15-ounce box that cost $1.89 and a package of 14 snack packs, each $\frac{1}{2}$ ounce, that cost $1.49. They had to figure out which was the better deal for the money. Third graders were asked to figure out how many chopsticks they'd need for all of the children in the class. In both instances, after talking about some possible ways to approach the problem, students wrote about their decisions and described their reasoning.

Also useful is to have class discussions about numerical strategies, with a focus on having students explain their reasoning, not just giving answers. Probe for different ways to figure. For example, in a fourth- or fifth-grade class, write a fraction on the board, such as $\frac{2}{3}$, and ask if it is more or less than $\frac{1}{2}$. Have students explain their thinking. After each response, ask, "Does anyone have another way to explain that?" In one fifth-grade class, Davy said, "There are three thirds in a whole, and $\frac{2}{3}$ is closer to a whole." Ramon volunteered, "On a measuring cup, the $\frac{2}{3}$ line is above the $\frac{1}{2}$ line." Leslie came to the board, drew a circle, and divided it into three equal-size wedges. She said, "You could cut a cookie into thirds like this. If you and a friend each take $\frac{1}{3}$, then you'd have to share some more to get $\frac{1}{2}$. So $\frac{1}{2}$ is $\frac{1}{3}$ plus some more." Rachel said, "If $\frac{2}{3}$ were the same as $\frac{1}{2}$, then 2 would have to be half of 3. But it's more, so $\frac{2}{3}$ has to be more." The discussion continued with $\frac{2}{3}$ until all students who wanted had a chance to explain. They played More or Less Than $\frac{1}{2}$ on other days with other fractions. When the teacher wrote $1\frac{1}{4}$ on the board one day, students blurted out that it was too easy. But even for an obvious problem, students may think in different ways.

It's also valuable for you to model different methods for computing. When children think that one way to compute is the "right" way, they focus on learning the method and applying it, rather than thinking about what makes sense for the situation. A one-way approach in the classroom doesn't help students learn to think flexibly. Think about figuring tips in restaurants. Few adults apply what they were taught in school—changing the percent into a decimal and multiplying, then following the rule for placing the decimal point in the answer. Instead, adults use a variety of different methods.

Include estimation in your instruction. As with other experiences that build number sense, estimation should be embedded in problem situations. Be wary of rounding-off exercises that focus on rules for rounding numbers. These don't promote number sense because they typically don't include contexts in which to make sense of the problem. For example, a teacher asked her students to time one minute on the class clock while she drew stars on the chalkboard. *(See Figure 4–2.)*

She then asked the children to think of different ways they could count the stars. The children suggested counting by 1s, by 2s, and by grouping the stars into 5s and 10s. They counted in each of these ways and found that they all produced the same result—the teacher had drawn 57 stars. "How many stars do you think I'd draw in just 30 seconds?" the teacher asked. After students gave and explained their estimates, she had them time 30 seconds while she drew stars again. Try this with your class. For older students, the estimation problem will be more of a challenge if you ask them to estimate how many stars you'll draw in 20, 25, 40 or some other number of seconds.

Problems involving measurement also help build number sense. Students can verify their estimates and calculations by actually measuring, which gives them a way to check their thinking in the physical world. This encourages children to take risks and try new ways of thinking. Young children, for example, enjoy exploring the lengths of different objects with interlocking cubes, estimating first and then measuring. They figure out each time how many cubes off they were and see if more experience helps them make closer estimates. Older children can use standard measuring units. For

**4–2.** Students time one minute while the teacher draws stars on the board.

**4-3.** Use adding machine tape, marked in one-inch intervals, to keep track of the number of days children come to school.

example, a class of fourth graders was keeping track of each day they were in school in anticipation of celebrating the one hundredth day. Each day, they marked a one-inch interval on a long strip of adding machine tape posted above the chalkboard. *(See Figure 4-3.)*

On the eleventh day of school they were given the problem of figuring out how long a strip of adding machine tape they'd need by the hundredth day. The students worked in pairs, using a variety of measuring tools—rulers, yardsticks, and tape measures. They predicted where on the classroom wall the "100 days" mark would be. Some students chose to adjust their predictions as the hundredth day approached.

|       | Using        |
| Five  | Manipulative |
|       | Materials    |

**K**athy, Liz, and Marielle signed up together for a workshop about using manipulative materials for teaching math. They each had some materials in their classrooms and the school was purchasing more for all of the teachers. Driving home, they talked about the day.

"It was a good day," Liz commented. "The workshop was jam-packed with activities. I have my favorites and I'm curious how the kids will take to them."

"What I'm thinking about is how to set up procedures to avoid chaos and confusion with materials," Kathy said. "I'm not sure if I should start with just one material or have the kids do some exploration with all of them."

"I'm wondering about how often we should be using materials in our math lessons," Marielle added.

"I hadn't thought about those things," Liz said. "But what I was wondering about was how to be sure that the parents see the materials as helping students learn math, that they're not just for playing."

Kathy, Liz, and Marielle were convinced that manipulatives could enable children to touch, feel, see, and make sense of mathematics. The workshop had given them a good start and lots of tips, and now they had to deal with specifics.

## 41 What are manipulative materials?

Manipulative materials are colorful, intriguing materials constructed to illustrate and model mathematical ideas and relationships and designed to be used by students in all grades. In classrooms across the nation you will find buckets of pattern blocks, trays of Cuisenaire rods, boxes of tiles and cubes, geoboards, tangrams, counters, dice, spinners, and more. Manipulative materials give children valuable and engaging first-hand experiences with mathematics. We can't imagine teaching math without them.

Many of us have visited a new town or city and felt confused about finding our bearings, even if we had a map and directions. After a few days, however, we have a feel for the area, and even if we get lost from time to time, we've learned some familiar landmarks and how they relate to one another. We're better able to find our way and can venture out with new confidence. We can think of the value of firsthand experiences for learning mathematics in a similar way. Math has many areas—number, geometry, measurement, statistics, probability, patterns, and more—and they're often unfamiliar, abstract, and confusing to students. We need to help children develop the ability and confidence to find their way around each of these areas, see relationships and make connections among them, and know what to do should they forget a fact or procedure.

A tall order? Perhaps. But that's the challenge teachers face for teaching mathematics. At every level from kindergarten on up, manipulative materials can help by providing students opportunities to get their hands—and also their minds—around abstract math ideas.

## 42 How can I help parents understand why manipulative materials are important for helping their children learn math? I worry that they think we're just playing during math time.

We've been asked this question many times and offer below five different reasons for using manipulative materials. You may want to communicate these to your students' families.

### 1. Manipulative materials give students a way to make abstract ideas concrete.

They say that a picture is worth a thousand words, but experience with the real thing is even more valuable. Young children learn to identify animals from picture books, but books don't give them a sense about animals' sizes, skin textures, or sounds. Even videos fall short. There's no substitute for firsthand experience, and manipulative materials increase students' learning by providing them ways to construct physical models of abstract mathematical ideas.

### 2. Manipulative materials lift math off textbook pages and give students a way to get their hands on ideas.

While we want students to become comfortable and proficient with the language of math—everything from the plus sign to notations of algebra—words and symbols only represent ideas. Ideas exist in children's minds, and manipulatives help children construct for themselves understanding of ideas that they can then connect to standard mathematical vocabulary and symbols.

**3. Manipulative materials build students' mathematical confidence by giving them a way to test and confirm their reasoning.**

Building student confidence with mathematics is key to children's future success, and what better way to build students' confidence with mathematics than to provide them with physical evidence to test their thinking. Materials help students investigate ideas in ways that make their understanding more robust.

**4. Manipulative materials are useful tools for solving problems.**

In searching for solutions, architects construct models of buildings, engineers build prototypes of equipment, and doctors use computers to predict the impact of medical procedures. In the same way in math class, manipulative materials serve as concrete models for students to use to find solutions to a wide variety of problems.

**5. Manipulative materials make learning math interesting and enjoyable.**

Give students the choice of working a page of problems or solving a problem with colorful and interestingly shaped blocks, and there's no contest. Manipulatives intrigue and motivate while helping students learn.

Along with explaining these ideas to parents, you may want to send home manipulatives for parents to explore. Include a suggestion for an investigation. Choose a material that the students have explored and learned with so that they can be the "expert" at home.

## 43 What guidelines should I set with my class about using manipulatives?

First of all, talk with your students about why manipulatives are valuable for learning math. Begin by giving the children time to explore a particular material. Then talk about what they noticed about the material and, perhaps, about the math concepts they'll be learning with it. Tell them why you think manipulative materials will help them learn math. (*See the ideas in the previous section, pages 52–53.*) Discussions like these are not only essential for first-time users but also useful refreshers to refocus students from time to time.

Next, be sure to set ground rules for how children should use materials. Discuss the similarities and differences between using math manipulatives in class and playing with toys or games at home. One difference is that when children play with toys at home, they're generally free to do what they like and often make up their own rules or find their own ways to play. In class, they'll be given specific suggestions and problems and activities to do with the materials. However, you want to encourage new discoveries and new ideas, so let the children know you're interested in their suggestions as well.

It's also important that students respect one another and not interfere when others are working with materials. At times, a student feels he or she must have just two more yellow color tiles and takes them from someone else's table, resulting in a howl of protest. In instances like these, take the time to interrupt the students and talk about the situation. You might even want to involve the entire class in the discussion.

Set up a system for storing materials and familiarize students with it. It's important that children know where materials are kept and how to store them. Some teachers designate and label space on bookshelves or in cabinets. Others use zip-top plastic bags and portion materials into quantities usable by pairs or small groups of students. Still others place a supply of each material at students' tables so they're always within reach. Whatever your system, it should be clear to students.

For easy reference, post a list of the materials in the classroom. A chart not only sends the message that you value the manipulatives but also helps students learn their names and how to spell them, which is useful for their written assignments. You may want to post other charts as well to record the shapes and colors of specific materials.

## 44 What tips do you have for classes that have never used manipulatives for math before?

Provide time for free exploration. Whenever you introduce a new material, you must provide time for the children to explore it and satisfy their curiosity, or they'll most likely get distracted from the task you assign. In a first experience, expect children to line up color tiles on their sides to see if they'll fall like dominoes, build tall towers with Cuisenaire rods, create large mosaics with pattern blocks, or construct houses, airplanes, or rockets out of interlocking cubes. This happens in classes at all grade levels.

After you've allowed time for free exploration, typically at least one full math period, ask students what they discovered about the materials. Record their observations on a chart to help them see that they learned something from their "play." Also, a class chart provides a vehicle for them to share their discoveries, which often provides others with new insights.

You may find that after you've allowed time for students to explore, they are still distracted by the materials. You may have given them a class period for exploration and now want them to focus on a specific problem or investigation, but they don't seem able to focus. This can be a struggle. One way to handle this is to tell them that you'll give them five minutes for their own exploration and then they will have to stop what they're doing and instead listen to the directions for what you want them to do. Doing this gives them a bit of time to satisfy their curiosity and ease into class.

An important note: Don't rely on teacher demonstrations for introducing materials. It's not enough to show the materials to students, let the students do the manipulating. Demonstrations alone are as limited as eating a papaya in front of the class and expecting the students to know how it tastes. Hands-on exploration is essential for students to discover relationships and construct their own understanding.

## 45 How often should I use manipulatives in my math teaching?

Use manipulative materials as often as they fit the lesson you've planned. Ideally, the materials should be available for students to use at any time as tools for helping them think, reason, and solve problems. Also, all students don't have to be using the same materials at the same time to solve a particular problem. They can seek out materials that they think will help them for a particular assignment. For example, fourth graders were given the problem of showing why $\frac{1}{2}$ plus $\frac{1}{4}$ was equal to $\frac{3}{4}$. Some pairs of students used color tiles. One pair built a three-by-four-tile rectangle that was half yellow, one-fourth blue, and the rest red, and then explained that the red part was worth $\frac{1}{4}$, which left $\frac{3}{4}$ for the other two parts. (*See Figure 5–1.*)

Another pair chose interlocking cubes, and built three trains using four, eight, and twelve cubes. As did the students who chose color tiles, they used different colors to show that $\frac{1}{2}$ plus $\frac{1}{4}$ was $\frac{3}{4}$ on each train. (*See Figure 5–2.*)

Several pairs of students drew or cut out circles to represent "pizzas" and divided them up to show $\frac{1}{2}$ plus $\frac{1}{4}$. (Paper and scissors are fine manipulatives and also tools students can use to model mathematical ideas.) The teacher had students report and then worked with the class to see how they might represent $\frac{1}{2}$ plus $\frac{1}{4}$ in other ways—using Cuisenaire rods, examining a measuring cup, and drawing on graph paper. They also explored with pattern blocks and decided that while useful for halves, thirds, and sixths, they didn't help with this problem. It's important for students to learn when a material is and isn't suitable for a problem or investigation.

| Y | Y | B | R |
|---|---|---|---|
| Y | Y | B | R |
| Y | Y | B | R |

**5–1.** Some students built a three-by-four rectangle with color tiles to show $\frac{1}{2}$ plus $\frac{1}{4}$ is equal to $\frac{3}{4}$.

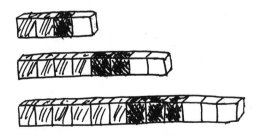

**5–2.** Others built trains with interlocking cubes.

At other times, however, a specific manipulative material is key to a lesson, and you'll initiate its use. First graders used pattern blocks for a lesson in sorting, classifying, and graphing. Each child took a two-handed scoop of blocks, sorted them by shape, and made a graph by placing shapes in separate columns on eighteen-by-twenty-four-inch newsprint ruled into a grid. (*See Figure 5–3.*)

The children then pasted construction paper shapes to make a permanent record of their graphs. The teacher posted one of the graphs and had the children talk about what they noticed. She posed questions:

Which block are there most of?

Which are there least of?

How many more green triangles are there than orange squares?

Which column has more—yellow hexagons or red trapezoids?

Over several days, she discussed all of the children's graphs. She then had the children take their graphs home and, with the help of a family member, write three sentences about what the graph showed. This allowed parents to see one way that manipulative materials were used in the class.

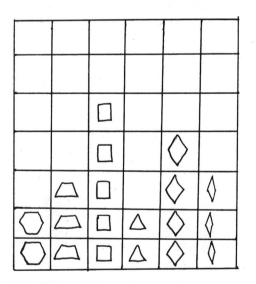

**5–3.** Students sort pattern blocks into a graph on an eighteen-by-twenty-four-inch piece of newsprint that has been ruled into a grid.

## 46 What about cutting paper into shapes—can't paper be seen as a manipulative, and a much cheaper one than wooden or plastic blocks?

Yes, paper folding and cutting certainly can help children get their hands on math and learn important mathematical ideas. It's valuable, for example, to have students cut construction paper squares into the seven pieces of the tangram puzzle, which convinces them that the pieces actually can be put back together to make a square. (*See Figure 5–4.*)

Also, children can cut paper "cookies" to explore fractions, fold paper shapes to learn about geometry, and use paper strips to learn about measurement.

But for investigations that involve students in using the pieces over and over again, paper just doesn't hold up and students get frustrated. Tangram puzzles made of plastic, for example, are valuable for investigations that follow the initial paper-cutting experience. Commercially produced manipulative materials are long-lasting, precise in ways that children's paper materials often aren't, and more inviting, and they give students the opportunity to discover the mathematical relationships inherent in them.

## 47 How many different materials do I need? Can I start with just one or two materials?

When you first introduce manipulatives in your classroom, or if you're just learning about the usefulness of materials, it makes sense to start with just one or two materials and provide students the chance to explore them in depth. But one of the advantages of a variety of materials is that children have the opportunity to think about the same ideas in different ways. Just as we want children to realize

**5–4.** The seven-piece tangram puzzle is cut from a square.

that fractions can be represented by things other than round "pies," we want them to learn to think flexibly about other mathematical ideas in several ways.

Top on our list of favorites for any grade level are easily available standards—pattern blocks, Cuisenaire rods, color tiles, geoboards, interlocking cubes (Unifix, Multilink, or Snap cubes), and tangrams. Pattern blocks are carefully constructed so children can compare the areas and perimeters of various polygons; they're useful for explorations about geometry, measurement, fractions, and more. In the same way, Cuisenaire rods are a time-honored favorite that help young children develop a sense of quantity through measuring and comparing as opposed to merely counting; older students use them to learn about fractions, measurement, functions, and more. Color tiles are one-inch squares that have the versatility to be used just as counters as well as for investigations in geometry, measurement, patterns, multiplication, and more. Similarly, interlocking cubes are also useful as counters and in other investigations and open up the world of three-dimensional geometry. Tangrams have delighted people for many years, and they engage children of all ages. Never turn down a supply of other materials, but look for these as basics.

## 48 I don't have enough of any material to use with my whole class. What can I do?

Teachers have solved this problem in various ways. Some organize learning centers, setting out the materials and having the children visit centers as space allows. Others introduce several activities for students to do over several days. Their choices, in part, are based on which materials are available. Some teachers pool materials with other teachers so that they have a class set for a week of instruction, after which they have fewer materials available for students to use individually or in small groups. In all cases, having students work cooperatively when they use materials not only cuts down on the amount of material you need but also encourages the kind of communication that promotes learning.

## 49 I know that manipulatives can help my slower learners, but do my better math students really need them?

Absolutely. The challenge of teaching any subject is to find learning activities that are accessible to all learners and, at the same time, have the richness to challenge the more interested or capable students. Manipulative materials are a wonderful resource for this.

For example, fourth graders learning about fractions were given the problem of finding all the different combinations of pattern blocks that could be used to build a yellow hexagon. (*See Figure 5–5.*)

This challenge was within the reach of all of the students, and all were able to record their constructions with correct fractional notation; the teacher had previously introduced how to write fractions. The few students who finished more quickly were offered an extension: *How much larger is the red trapezoid than the blue parallelogram?* This problem asked them to figure out how much more $\frac{1}{2}$ was than $\frac{1}{3}$. Extensions are useful for making lessons appropriate for students at all levels.

**I know that older students benefit from using manipulatives, but I worry they'll complain that the materials are too babyish. Do you have any hints for this?**

50

You most likely won't get this initial reaction from older students. Most are delighted to have the opportunity to get their hands on some concrete material, and resistors get involved easily. But if you anticipate some resistance, you might talk about the importance of modeling to helping solve mathematical problems, the way architects and engineers build prototypes. Tell the students that they'll have the opportunity to use materials in a similar way to model mathematical situations and solve problems.

Even if you don't get resistance, our advice is to make the first experience something that serves the purpose of offering a challenge. It's important that students see the materials as dealing with math at their level. A caution: even if this is the first time older students are using materials, you'll need to provide time for them to explore the material.

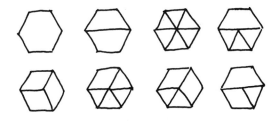

**5–5.** Students found different ways to use pattern blocks to construct the yellow hexagon.

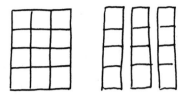

**5–6.** Using rectangles built with color tiles, students can see how 3 × 4 means three groups of four.

## 51 What can I do for students who can do what I ask with the materials but still have trouble with textbook work?

Children do not automatically make connections between the work they do with manipulative materials and the corresponding mathematics represented abstractly. Children tend to think that the manipulations they do with models are one method for finding a solution and pencil-and-paper math is entirely separate. One of the important challenges in math teaching is to help students make connections.

For example, while it may be obvious to adults, it's not so for students to see how a three-by-four-inch rectangle they built with color tiles relates to "3 times 4" or the explanation in the textbook that "3 × 4 means three groups of four." (*See Figure 5–6.*)

Teachers need to make those connections, to show how a rectangle can be separated into three rows with four tiles in each and to talk about how the rectangle is another way to show three groups of four. Connecting concrete experiences to the standard symbolism of mathematics is an essential aspect of teaching.

Also, when doing textbook work, if the textbook doesn't reference any manipulative material, talk with the students about what they might use to help. Often, students don't realize that something they use in one setting can be helpful in another.

# Six

# Dealing with Calculators

The issue of using calculators in math class came up at a staff meeting, and the talk was about establishing a schoolwide policy. "It's important that the students are aware of their use and purpose," Shelley, the principal, said. "They're not a substitute for learning to think on their own."

Some of the teachers at Penny's table expressed confusion. Penny raised her hand. "Should they be available to students all of the time?" "What about kids bringing their own from home?" Adria added. "Then they're all different."

"Those are important issues to discuss," Shelley said. She wrote the questions on chart paper and turned back to the faculty. "Let's list other questions you have and then tackle them one by one."

Calculators are valuable tools for math instruction. But as with any teaching tool, it's important to think about how best to incorporate calculators into your instructional program.

## 52 Should I let my students use calculators? If so, when?

Calculators are real-world tools that can be used effectively in any math program. Think about when you use a calculator. Most likely you rely on it as a labor-saving device when a calculation is complex and you want to be sure to be correct. Of course human error is possible with a calculator, but it's quick and easy to redo a calculation on a calculator to check for accuracy.

Students should learn how to use calculators, and we advise that calculators be readily available in your classroom. But we also want students to develop the understanding and skills necessary to solve computation problems mentally and with paper and pencil. This means that there are times when you won't want your students to use calculators. Children should be able to do simple calculations in their heads without relying on calculators—or on paper and pencil, either. Also, if you're assessing your students' ability to calculate or you want them to practice computing, then it's fine to tell them not to use a calculator or to use a calculator but also to do the computation without a calculator and explain how they figured. When you decide that you don't want students to use calculators in a specific situation, however, be sure to let them know the reason for your decision.

For example, some students were playing Pig. The goal of the game is to be the first to score at least 100 points. Players take turns rolling two dice and keeping a running total of the sums that come up. On a round, a player rolls as many times as he or she likes, records the total, and adds it to the scores from previous rounds. But, if a 1 comes up on one of the dice before the player decides to stop rolling, the player scores 0 for that round. Even worse, if a 1 comes up on *both* dice, not only does the turn end but the player's entire accumulated total returns to 0. The game is a favorite for students from grade three on. After a teacher introduced the game to fourth graders, Brian asked, "Can we use calculators?" "No," the teacher responded. "One of the benefits of the game is the practice you get adding mentally. Don't use a calculator, and be sure to check one another's calculations as you play." The teacher was clear and the students were fine with the decision.

## 53 How can I best teach children how to use a calculator?

The best way to learn about any new tool is to use it for a real purpose. Pose investigations for the children that familiarize them with calculators. Aside from being a useful tool for computing, calculators can also enhance children's numerical understanding and help develop their number sense.

For example, third graders investigated patterns in whole-number addition problems. They were shown how to use the "=" key for repeated additions. After pressing "2 + 2 =" and checking that 4 was on the display, the children pressed "=" again and again and noted the pattern of numbers that appeared: 6, 8, 10, 12, . . . . (Note: This won't work with calculators that don't have a repeating addition feature. If your calculator continues to show 4 instead of 4, 6, 8, 10, and so on, then it won't be useful for this activity.) They repeated this for "3 + 2 = = = . . ." and "2 + 3 = = = . . . ." They tried other combinations and wrote about what they discovered. They did a similar activity for subtraction—for example, "20 – 4 = = = . . ."—investigating combinations of "starting" and "minus" numbers that got to 0 and those that didn't.

Sixth graders used the calculator for a similar number-sense investigation that involved decimals. The teacher introduced the activity by having the students press ".5," then "+," then "=" and "=" again. The students verified that they got a 1 on the display.

Their challenge was to try other starting numbers, press "+," and then press "=" as many times as necessary to see if they could land exactly on 1. They were to find as many starting numbers as possible that got to 1 in this way.

While older students most likely have already learned how to do calculations on a calculator, young children may need help. A class of second graders was solving problems that called for combining and comparing numerical quantities. One of the activities was to estimate first and then count the number of popcorn kernels that filled a Unifix cube; a piece of tape was put over the bottom of the cube so the kernels wouldn't spill out. About to figure out how far off her estimate was, Rachel came up to the teacher, calculator in hand. "What do I push?" she asked. An important goal of math instruction is for children to interpret problem situations, decide which operation is appropriate, and do the calculation correctly. Asking "what to push" indicated either that Rachel wasn't sure what to do or she didn't know how to use the calculator. The teacher asked, "How might you solve the problem without a calculator?" Rachel replied, "I'd do subtraction," and then, "Oh, yeah." She skipped back to her seat and got out paper and pencil. Later the teacher showed her how to subtract with a calculator to check her answer.

## 54 The students in my class bring their own calculators to school, so they all have different kinds. What should I do about dealing with the differences?

We don't think that it's necessary, or even preferred, to have all identical calculators available in class. We'd actually rather have a variety. After all, children will encounter all sorts of calculators outside of school, and they might as well get used to dealing with an assortment in class.

Encourage children to bring calculators from home. In class, have the students pair up and compare similarities and differences between their calculators. You might suggest the following questions to begin their comparisons:

How many digits can be shown on the display?

Do they have the same keys or are their differences?

How do the arrangements of the keys compare?

Do they both have memories?

Try a subtraction problem where the second number is larger than the first; for example, 4 – 7. Do your calculators give the same answer?

Do your calculators give the same answer to 2 ÷ 3?

What other differences can you find?

You may want to pair up students differently and repeat the activity so that they have a chance to explore other calculators. Then initiate a class discussion so students can share what they discovered.

We have one caution, however: Even though we recommend that you encourage students to bring their calculators from home, it's extremely important that you're sensitive to the possibility that some children might not be able to do so. Be sure that you have enough calculators on hand so that every child has access to one. Assuring equity in this regard is essential so that no children are made to feel deficient if they don't have a calculator of their own, and your awareness in this area is required.

## Seven | Incorporating Writing into Math Class

**A**t lunch one day, Naomi brought up a problem she was having. "My class seems to be doing fine during math lessons and our discussions are getting better. At least the kids seem to be listening to each other better. But when I ask them to write about their ideas so I can get a sense of what's going on inside each of their heads, many of them fall apart. And even if they aren't falling apart, they do a lot of complaining."

Dolores expressed her thoughts. "Writing has been a struggle for me, too. I think the class is getting better at it, though they still gripe, but what worries me is sending home papers that have spelling and grammar errors. When they're writing in math, I'm not so concerned with *how* they write as with *what* they write. But parents get upset when papers have mistakes."

Others at the table had suggestions. "Writing has been easier in my class since I've had the kids keep math journals," Tom said. "When I have my students write letters to explain their thinking, it seems to work better," Jessica said. But they, too, had questions. How do you respond to students' writing? Do you correct what they write on each assignment? What kind of feedback is most useful? How do you get them to edit their work? They all agreed that writing was important, especially for preparing students for the writing they had to do on the districtwide math test, but they all felt that they needed help.

## 55 How can I get my students to explain their work and their answers in writing?

We know that children learn to speak long before they can read or write. It makes sense, then, that in order for children to communicate their thoughts in writing, they first need to be able to explain their ideas verbally. But remember that helping students learn to give concise, clear, and organized verbal explanations takes time. Class discussions help encourage students to explain their thinking, and students need to sense that their responses will be welcomed and listened to. (*For help with leading discussions, see Chapter 3.*)

To begin, give writing assignments immediately following class discussions. Encourage children to write just as if they were speaking to the class or to a partner, getting the words they can say onto their papers. To offer assistance when students are having difficulty writing, ask questions:

What did you think or do first?

What did you do right after that?

What helped you sense that your answer was reasonable?

If a student is having difficulty explaining verbally, enlist support from classmates. Ask if someone else can help explain first and then give the child another try. As children become more comfortable explaining, they move closer to being able to communicate effectively through writing.

It also helps to remind students why their writing is important, that it both promotes their learning and helps you teach them better. Let them know that you're deeply interested in what each of them is learning, and because it's not possible to hear everyone's ideas every day in the classroom, their writing helps give you an inside look into their thinking.

## 56  Is it useful for students to keep a math notebook, journal, or log?

First of all, consider the reasons for children to keep math notebooks. For starters, writing can enhance math learning. It pushes children to examine and express their thinking. We also know that writing is useful in math to keep track of thinking, especially when ideas or calculations are too complex to keep straight in our heads. And it's helpful for making sense when you're reading math books. When reading math, you have to think about the ideas presented to understand what's being described or explained, and writing is often the best tool for doing so. In general, writing is an extremely important tool for learning math.

For these reasons, we think it's good for you to involve your students in writing as they learn. We've learned about and used different methods with different classes. While we don't think that there's a best system for writing in math, here are some options for you to consider and see what fits your preferences and purposes.

Some teachers like each child to have a math notebook or to keep a math journal or math log. In some classes, children do all of their class work in their notebooks, using them on a daily basis during lessons to keep notes about what occurs and to do problems. Some teachers ask children to write daily entries at the end of math class describing what they did that day and what they learned, including things they're not sure about or questions they have about the math they're studying. Some teachers, however, only have students use their notebooks for particular class assignments, such as when they give the students a problem to do or raise a question for them to reflect on. Your decision about how you'll use notebooks should depend on your purposes, your preferences, and the particular ages and needs of your students.

## 57 Do you have any tips for managing students' math notebooks in the classroom?

Ah, the management question. It's an important one. Much of the success of a class depends on the organizational systems we set up to make learning possible. Following are some tips teachers have reported to us that we've tried and found to be successful.

First of all, there are many options for what students can use as journals. Some teachers give students small bound notebooks that the school makes available. Other teachers have children supply their own. In some classes, children make their journals, using a twelve-by-eighteen-inch piece of construction paper for the cover and stapling paper inside. Some teachers feel that they'd rather have the children use loose paper for assignments than work in a notebook or log, and they give them a folder for keeping their work. These teachers say that it's hard to page through notebooks to find each child's work on a particular assignment and also that it's easier to take home a set of papers than lug all of their journals around. Still, some of these teachers report that they use bound journals for daily reflections and children's questions. One third-grade teacher told us that when children wanted a response to some question they raised in their math journal, they put in a bookmark made from a strip of construction paper or a Post-it Note as a signal. She was sure to read and respond to those journals each day. She used this bookmark system for children's personal journals as well.

We also have some logistical tips. Some teachers set guidelines for their students to make entries easier to find—a date and title at the top of each page, for example. With regard to storage, some teachers feel it's best to keep students' math journals in class at all times to avoid children forgetting them at home or losing them. When math class begins, one child distributes them. To make filing and distributing easy, some teachers have children use a large marker to write their names at the top of the cover. Some teachers reported also assigning a number to each child, usually in order alphabetically by first names, so that it's easy to file journals in a box and also to check to see if any are missing.

If you decide to use journals, think through the options before making your decisions. Be sure to clarify the purpose and guidelines to your students. Sometimes a system you try turns out not to work as smoothly as you'd like. In that case, make changes as you see fit. What's most important is that the system you adopt serves the students' learning and your ability to assess their progress.

## 58 I'm interested in examples of how teachers actually use math journals in their classes. Can you give some ideas?

A second-grade teacher reported that her students began math class each day by writing the date in their journals and then five number sentences that represented the day of the month. A sixth-grade teacher told us that when her students were studying quadrilaterals, she asked them to write about why a square was a special kind of rectangle. In a third-grade class, the children reported the results of their data-gathering homework assignment—how many times their telephone rang the night before between 6 P.M. and 8 P.M.—by writing their data on Post-its that they organized into a graph on the board. Before discussing the graph, each student individually wrote in his or her journal the conclusions he or she drew from the posted data. In another class, after deciding that there were approximately 28 beans in one scoop, fourth-grade students were asked to figure out about how many beans were in a jar that held 12 scoops. They were asked to solve the problem in two different ways as a check that their answer was reasonable.

Teachers who have their students write daily reflections reported a variety of ways of doing so. A first-grade teacher made math logs of stapled sheets of paper for her students. She duplicated sheets with a space at the top of each for the date, which gave the children practice writing it. And there were two prompts:

Today I did _____.
Today I learned _____.

The children were encouraged to use words, numbers, and/or pictures to complete them. A third-grade teacher told us she did the same thing but also had a space for the time at the top of the page to give children practice with reading the clock and recording the time. For older students, teachers didn't prepare pages ahead of time but reported success with giving prompts. Sample prompts are:

What I know about _____ so far is _____.
What I'm still not sure about is _____.
What I'd like to know more about is _____.

Teachers also give assignments from their texts and ask the students to do the work in their journals.

## 59 What's a good system for keeping track of student work?

Whether you have your students keep math journals, write on separate sheets of paper, or both, it's essential that you have a system for keeping track of and filing students' work so that you can assess their progress. One way we've found to be efficient and effective is to set up a file box with a folder for each child. Separate from the box of journals or the children's work folders, which they use on a daily basis, this is for keeping samples of work that will, over time, give you a chronological record of each child's work. You don't need to put every piece of work a student does in his or her folder, but you should include those items that give insights into the child's thinking, reasoning, understanding, and skills. Having folders of students' work is a real boon to parent conferences when you can together take a look at children's growth and identify their needs.

What about work that gets sent home and, therefore, isn't in the folder? If a set of papers is useful for assessing students, but you want to send it home, make copies for their folders first. Or choose not to send some papers home and, instead, file them to review with parents later. A suggestion: If you've never tried saving children's work like this, you might begin by saving all of the children's math papers for three or four weeks. Then, after a month, look through the files and see which papers give you insights into their understanding and which don't. This will help you make choices later about what's valuable to save. There's no rule about how many papers to keep, but you might think about one a week being a general average.

Also, you may find it useful at times to have your students look through their folders and think about their learning. Some schools include students in parent conferences, and this is a good way to help you and the students prepare for them. (*See chapter 10 about parent conferences.*) Examining work with your students is a way to help them celebrate their learning and involve them more in their own learning process.

## 60 What about worksheets— when do you use these?

Worksheets have long been standards in math instruction. They seem to be a quick and easy solution for preparing children's assignments. The problems are organized and it's generally clear where and how children are to respond. While it may seem to you that children's work will be better organized when done on worksheets, or perhaps easier for you to decipher, we advise that you don't rely on them and instead give children the responsibility and opportunity to organize their work on paper in their own ways.

Think about what you do when preparing a worksheet. Not only do you think about the content of the mathematics, but you also decide how to set up and organize the page, and then you prepare it. Students benefit from having to think about and organize assignments for themselves. Also, when students organize their own work, they're not constrained by the particular way you chose to present the assignment. As an example, a teacher wanted her sixth graders to learn about π and asked them to measure and compare the circumference and diameter of at least ten circular objects. She modeled how to do this with her coffee cup, recording the numbers on the chalkboard and then dividing to see how many times larger the circumference was than the diameter. Rather than preparing a worksheet with a chart on which they would record their data, she asked them to think about how they would collect and present their work to communicate clearly what they were doing and learning. Later she talked with the class about the different ways students organized the assignment.

It may be more time-consuming to have students work without worksheets, but the experience makes a valuable contribution to their learning. We're big on having students take this responsibility and limiting our use of worksheets. However, we do provide children a variety of paper on which to work—lined paper; blank paper; squared paper with squares of different sizes; triangle paper, which is good for working with pattern blocks; dot paper, which is good for working with geoboards and also for fractions and area problems; 0–99 and 1–100 charts for exploring number patterns; and more.

## 61 I've been pushing my students to write more complete explanations when they're solving problems. How should I react to their work?

When reading students' papers, keep two purposes in mind. One is to learn more about each individual student, adding on to the information you already have. Another is to get a broad sense of the overall class response in order to evaluate the lesson. And each purpose suggests different issues to consider.

To learn more about individual students, for example, when you read their papers think about questions like the following:

Is the answer correct?

Did the student include the reasoning that supports the solution?

If computation was required, did the student use an efficient method and/or mental math?

If appropriate to the problem, does the solution indicate use of estimation or anticipation of the magnitude of the answer?

What would you still like to know about the child's thinking or response, even after evaluating the paper?

When looking to evaluate the effectiveness of the lesson, think about questions like these:

Was the assignment accessible to all students?

Was it also an appropriate challenge for the more able students?

Would I assign it again to another class? Were there common misconceptions?

Were there unique responses from which other students might benefit?

What might subsequent lessons offer?

A class set of papers can provide information that's invaluable for future planning.

In either situation, a good way to react to students' work is to devote class time for discussing a particular assignment they've done. This helps you set the tone for the students about your expectations for their work. Focus on how their papers help you learn what they do and don't understand. Stress to them that the more detail they provide, the better their papers communicate to you. Sometimes it helps to read aloud one or two papers—either with permission from the students or anonymously—as models of papers that were particularly useful for helping you understand how students reasoned. Point out why they helped.

As part of a unit about measuring area and perimeter, for example, each student in a fifth-grade class was given the assignment of tracing one of his or her feet onto centimeter-squared paper and approximating its area. (*See Figure 7–1.*)

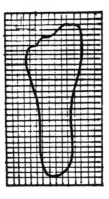

**7–1.** Students traced one of their feet on centimeter-squared paper and figured its area.

The assignment included writing a description of how the students arrived at their answers. These students were new to writing in math class and the quality of their papers varied widely. To help them think more about writing, it was useful to read aloud several of the papers, withholding their names, and have students talk about them. For each, the teacher asked several questions:

Was the explanation clear?

If so, what made it clear?

What more do you need to know?

After discussing three papers in this way, the teachers gave the students their papers back for revision. The teacher reminded them why their writing was important, that this was a beginning assignment, and that with practice their writing would improve.

One more thought: It's helpful to save students' written responses and begin a filing system to keep track of individual students' work. Then both you and your students can review their progress over time. (*See page 69 for information about filing student work.*)

## 62 Should I make notes when I read students' work so that I can remember what's important?

Whether you make written notes when reading students' work is a matter of your own personal preference and the amount of time that you have available. If you choose to jot down notes when reading a class set of papers, write your reactions on Post-it Notes rather than marking on children's papers. This can be less intimidating to students, especially if you're asking them to revise their work. After you've reviewed all of their papers, skim your Post-it Notes. Look for things that cropped up over and over again, such as a common error or method of reasoning, and consider bringing it up in the next day's lesson for a class discussion. If you have concerns or questions for one child or just a few children, however, find a spare moment during the day to clarify misconceptions with them. Your notes will help you recall what you were thinking at the time, so you won't have to retrace your thoughts.

Don't feel you have to give students individual comments on all of their papers. Not only would this be overwhelming to do for all the papers your students turn in, but it's also unnecessary when students are in the process of learning. The time to give individual feedback is when you're assessing individual progress, not using students' work to help you make the best instructional decisions possible.

When you decide to give individual reactions, avoid general comments such as "Good job" or "Nice thinking." These don't offer the child any real valuable feedback. Your feedback should respond specifically to what they wrote. Address the mathematics in the task, indicate your interest in how they think and reason, or offer suggestions for further thinking. Even better, arrange time to talk with students about their work.

## 63 If I don't have time to give specific feedback to children's papers, isn't it okay, or even better, to indicate "good job" or "nice thinking" or some other general comment than to say nothing?

Of course we want our students to feel a sense of success and accomplishment. But you need to empower children to feel pleased with themselves, rather than to rely on you to fuel their self-images. When you praise students with statements such as "good work" or "I like what you've done," you send a message to them that they will not know the value of their work without your praise. Naturally, you want children to know that their actions and products are valued. But you don't want them to think that you are always passing judgment on their work or that you or other adults are the sole decision makers in categorizing work or actions as good or bad. We realize that you don't have time to write lengthy and detailed comments on every set of student work. Our view is that if you don't have time to respond with specifics, then no comment is better than a generic one.

However, we don't mean to imply that we ignore children's work. There are other ways to give feedback that supports continued learning. For example, after reading a set of papers, begin class the next day by telling the students what you noticed and use it as a springboard for a discussion or new exploration. You might say, "Several of you thought that. . . ." Or, "A few of you figured that. . . ." Or you could read something from an individual's paper. In this case, we recommend you ask permission first. If a student is reticent, spend some time with the student to understand his or her concerns. Giving feedback in this way emphasizes that the work that children do on assignments is important, not only to help you learn about their thinking but also to help you plan lessons that better meet their learning needs.

Another way for students to receive feedback is for them to discuss their work in small groups. Post a general question for groups to discuss, such as:

Did you agree on the answers?

What different ways did you use to solve the problems?

Or pose to the group some variation of the assignment:

What would happen if you tried this with different numbers (or different shapes or different data)?

Try your different methods on this similar problem and see if you get the same answer.

Which method would you choose for this problem?

Giving students a related assignment to work on helps them make connections and see relationships among activities, practice skills in different situations, or apply different approaches to a problem. And group discussions can help students revisit and extend their learning experiences.

## 64 A friend has her students write letters to explain their reasoning so that they feel their writing in math class has purpose. What do you think about this idea?

Letters give children an audience for their writing. In general it's important to establish yourself as the audience for the students' writing and give the students enough experience with getting feedback from you that they know that you really do read and think about what they write. Letters to others, however, is a good alternative and can give assignments a fresh appeal.

Sometimes letter-writing assignments can be real, directed to someone the children actually know or who would be interested in the information. In these cases, students can actually mail or deliver the letters and, perhaps, get responses. One teacher reported that she had her sixth graders conduct a comparison of several different brands of raisin bread, figuring out the average number of raisins in a slice. They wrote letters presenting their findings to the company whose brand had the most and also to their parents to lobby for future purchases. In their letters, they described the experiment they did and provided the data they collected. Another teacher, as part of a unit on multidigit multiplication, asked his fourth graders to figure out how old they would be on their next birthday in months, weeks, days, and hours. He asked them to write a letter to a family member and explain how they figured it out and to offer to figure out the reader's age in this way for him or her. Some children thought it would be good to make birthday cards for others giving them the information about their age in months, weeks, days, and hours. In both cases the activity went well and the students' letters were detailed and animated.

Assignments can also ask students to write "imaginary" letters. For example, when students are learning something new, it can help to have them write letters explaining the idea to students one grade below, students new to class, or students who had been absent for a while. In his book *Writing to Learn*, William Zinsser writes: "Writing is a way to work yourself into a subject and make it your own" (1988, 16). You might ask third graders, as an example, to explain to a second grader what multiplication is and how to find answers to single-digit multiplication problems. You might ask second graders to write the rules for a math game they learned so that a student in another class could play it. You might ask sixth graders to explain to a fifth grader why a triangle can't have two right angles.

One caution: When you have students write letters that will actually get delivered, we think you should give attention to their grammar and punctuation, something you might not be too concerned about for assignments that only you will read. Give your feedback and then ask students to edit their letters before you accept them as final. (*See page 76 for comments about children's grammar and punctuation.*)

## 65 No matter how much practice my students have with writing, they still grumble and resist when I give a writing assignment. How should I respond to their complaints?

This isn't an unusual situation. Grumbling and resisting is usually a sign that the children don't feel comfortable doing what you've asked and, therefore, aren't willing to try. To address this situation, it helps to regularly remind students why their writing is important and valuable—to them and to you—and what you expect. Give the guidelines often and keep them brief. Here's a sample reminder: "Remember that your writing helps you revisit and clarify your thinking, which will help you learn. Also, your writing gives me information that I use to plan lessons that help you learn." You'll know that you've given the message a sufficient number of times when you hear students parrot it back.

Of course, this won't necessarily stop the grumbling, especially for reluctant writers. When children are having difficulty with a particular assignment, take time to have them explain their thinking to you. Say, "Tell me your idea," or "Tell me what you're thinking." When the child gets out a sentence or two, stop him or her and say, "Let's start by writing down what you just said." After the student does this, ask him or her to read the sentences aloud and then say, "Tell me more about what you were thinking." Then get the child started writing again. In this way, we've had good success coaxing children into writing a fairly complete paper and arriving at a satisfying product. Sometimes when the class is working on an assignment, it helps to sit by a child having difficulty so you're near enough to prompt and keep the child on task, while also dealing with other children's needs from there.

Another thing you might try is to give all of the students the same assignment and use it for a class discussion. For an accessible assignment, ask them to describe in writing what they did on an activity, as opposed to describing how they were thinking about a problem. Writing about thinking is harder than describing a more concrete action. As an example, second graders were filling Unifix cubes, which had been taped on the bottom to cover the hole, with popcorn kernels and lentils. They were estimating how many of each would fit in a cube, filling the cube, and then seeing how far off their estimates were. Their teacher asked them to describe what they had done so their parents would understand how they were learning to estimate, measure, and think about numbers. Some wrote detailed descriptions; others wrote brief descriptions. The teacher chose a few papers to read aloud, keeping them anonymous, and asked the others to listen to see if they would really know what the student had done and, if not, to suggest what each student could add to his or her paper to provide more details. In this way, the children got an idea of the thoroughness the teacher expected from their papers. The time was well spent for helping the children see what the teacher was looking for and how they might accomplish it.

However, even capable writers will complain. Because we feel that having students write is so important to their math learning, our advice is to hang in there and push. Prod them to use words, numbers, and pictures to make their thinking as explicit as possible. We feel as if we're nagging when we do this, and we are. But we nag anyway.

## 66 On some of the children's writing assignments in math, the spelling and grammar errors are glaring. Should I have students correct mistakes before I send their papers home?

This is a question we've been asked many, many times. It's a big issue. When we're focused on teaching math, of course we also pay attention to students' learning in other areas—their reading and writing skills, citizenship, work habits, and so on. Children's written work, however, is the aspect of math class that's most visible and, therefore, the most open for scrutiny. There's nothing worse than an irate parent calling to complain about the poor quality of his or her child's writing on papers that come home. We've heard different views about dealing with this issue, and there's some logic in each of them.

Some teachers, for example, say that the primary purpose of having children write in math class is for them to clarify their reasoning, reflect on ideas, and express how they think. Having children correct every error puts the emphasis on their writing ability instead of their mathematical thinking. Also, asking children to correct all of their writing errors, some teachers argue, will stifle them or, worse yet, turn them off from writing in math class.

Other teachers say, however, that learning to write correctly is an extremely important aspect of children's education, that we're not serving children well enough if we allow their papers with errors to go uncorrected. They feel that a paper worth writing is worth writing well. Correcting papers should be an accepted routine in class, even in math class.

Some teachers counter this argument. If you're writing for publication, they say, then of course it's important to edit your work. However, when the purpose of writing is for students to work their way into understanding or to reveal to the teacher how they're thinking, the writing falls into a different category. People generally don't correct their spelling and grammar in diaries, and this is more like reflective diary writing, they say.

Other teachers counter the argument differently. Keep the focus on the coherence, clarity, and thoroughness of students' ideas, they say. When students' papers are muddled or incomplete, then it's important to talk with them about their thinking and, after such a conversation, ask them to do a revision. But while revising is important as a way to support math learning, it's less important to edit errors that don't detract from the meaning.

One teacher told us that she had a stamp made that read "Uncensored Children's Work." She informed parents that this stamp indicated that she knew there were errors, either grammatical or spelling, but that she wasn't using this particular paper to focus on those skills. She was, however, very concerned with their writing and would be working on writing skills throughout the year. For papers that she stamped, she urged parents to look at the ideas the child was presenting and bypass, for the moment, the writing mistakes.

Ideally, this is an issue that would be good to discuss with the other teachers in your school so that there's consistency among all classes and, therefore, among the expectations of parents.

## 67 What's a portfolio? Should I have my students create math portfolios?

A common use of portfolios is for people to show a sampling of their best work. Artists and photographers, for example, generally have portfolios to display their work. Bakeries sometimes have photographs of cakes available for special occasions. In these examples, portfolios are like resumés. In classrooms, however, teachers use portfolios in a variety of ways. Following are three possible classroom applications.

As they do for artists and bakeries, portfolios in the classroom can provide samples of children's best work. A fourth-grade teacher told us that she saves children's work in all subject areas and works with the students to select a few pieces to send home with report cards. She feels that the actual work helps give parents insights into their child's accomplishments in a way that grades alone can't. The children write about the work they select, explaining why they chose it and what it particularly shows. The teacher adds her comments as well.

Some teachers don't link portfolios to report card periods but instead use them after completing a unit as a way for students to reflect on what they learned as well as to communicate with their parents. Some teachers report that they give the students guidelines for selecting work samples to include. Criteria can include the following: best work, favorite paper, a paper that describes a mathematical discovery, or a paper about an idea you're still wondering about or unsure of. Students explain the reasons for their choices in a cover letter for their portfolio.

Other teachers, however, prefer that portfolios be used as indicators of students' progress over time rather than as samples of their best work. Having a folder of children's work arranged chronologically is especially useful for parent conferences to provide concrete examples of children's learning and needs.

If your school doesn't have a specific policy about portfolios, and you'd like to try using them to help children think about their learning and communicate about their schooling with their families, team with another teacher to plan for this. It's good to have some professional support as you think through your decisions.

# Eight

Linking

Math

and

Literature

"**H**ere's the book I told you about that I used to introduce geometry," Linda said to Paolo. "It was a terrific kickoff for the unit."

Paolo thanked Linda. When Linda was talking about how she incorporated children's literature throughout the year for math instruction, he had asked her what she used. The book looked interesting to him, but he thought to himself, "Why would I want to read a book during math class? Aren't my kids better off doing math during math time and reading during reading time?" Still, he respected Linda and was willing to give it a try. He wanted to help his students see connections among the different subjects they studied.

## 68 Why is it valuable to spend math instructional time using children's books?

Using children's books in math instruction serves several purposes. One is, of course, to support math learning, and children's books do this in several ways. They can introduce children to new mathematical ideas, provide opportunities for them to think in new ways about concepts they've already studied, and provide contexts for them to practice math skills.

Also, stories help children experience math through books other than textbooks. Stories that engage and delight can make mathematical ideas accessible, interesting, even compelling for children. And along with the mathematical benefits, children's books used in math class also contribute to developing children's love of books and reading. All in all, children's literature can make a significant contribution to children's math education.

Counting books provide the most obvious math-related reading. However, there are many other options that extend mathematics beyond counting. We're especially fond of books that offer good stories that are well told and imaginatively illustrated. We're always on the lookout for books that we consider to be good literature, that can be read and enjoyed for themselves, not only for their math potential. In fact, from talking with the authors of books we've found intriguing for math class, we've learned that many never had math in mind when they wrote their book! They've been generally surprised—and delighted—to learn how we use their books to support math learning.

If you haven't yet used children's books for math learning, you—and your students—are in for a treat. A suggestion: Don't immediately follow every book you read aloud with a math learning activity. Allow time for children to savor stories. Then come back to the book a second time. Ask children to recall the story and tell it in their own words. Then engage them in the mathematical activity you had planned.

Another suggestion: After reading a book, rather than presenting a problem for the students to solve, ask them to think about problems that relate to the story. This gives children the opportunity to pose problems that are interesting to them. Also, their ideas can help you assess their view of problem solving and the sorts of problems with which they're comfortable.

## 69 After I read a book to my class, there are always several children who want to borrow the book and take it home to share. How can I help parents use the book to its mathematical advantage?

Encouraging parents to have some positive math interaction with their children is important, and children's books provide a wonderful vehicle for doing so. The attention parents give when reading with their children is typically pleasurable and loving, and bringing math into reading time is a real plus. Children's books provide ways for parents to spend math time with their children other than dealing with homework at the kitchen table.

Some children's books include suggestions at the end of the book to help parents, teachers, or other adults engage children in the specific mathematical content in the book. If the book you're sending home doesn't do this, however, you may want to send home the work the student did in class as well so parents can see the related math learning. When you send home a book for children to share with their families, put the book in a zip-top plastic bag and include general guidelines for parents. Following is a suggestion for a letter you might enclose.

Dear Parent,

Reading the enclosed children's book with your child gives you the opportunity not only to support your child's love of reading and books but also to help develop your child's curiosity, interest, and appreciation of mathematics. You may find the following guidelines useful.

- Read the story aloud with your child, or have your child read it aloud to you, or read parts and invite your child to fill in missing parts or "read" important last words in a line.
- Some children when listening to stories may interrupt at times to express an idea or ask a question. Some may examine and talk about the colorful illustrations. Others, however, may listen intently until the end. All of these reactions are fine. Follow your child's lead.
- As with any book, reread it if your child is interested. Rereading can help children see the details, including the math content, more clearly.

Spending mathematics time with your child can help develop his or her mathematical interest and confidence. Enjoy reading and learning math with your child!

## 70  I can see how children's books are appropriate for young children, but I teach sixth graders. What sorts of books work for older students?

In our experience, older students enjoy being read to as much as do students in the early grades. While picture books are generally geared to younger children, we've found that even the simpler books often lead to mathematical investigations that are suitably complex for older students. *Anno's Mysterious Multiplying Jar* (Anno and Anno), for example, poses a math problem of how many jars there are in all. (The answer is 3,628,800.) The book introduces children to the idea and usefulness of factorial numbers. *A Million Fish . . . More or Less* (McKissack) also engages students in thinking about large numbers. Aileen Friedman's *A Cloak for the Dreamer* engages students in thinking about why geometric shapes do or don't tessellate. *One Hundred Hungry Ants*, by Elinor J. Pinczes, leads to a discussion of factors of one hundred. We even found *Annabelle Swift, Kindergartner* (Schwartz) to be engaging to sixth graders and useful for involving them with calculating mentally to figure out how much milk money Annabelle counted.

Some chapter books, while they don't deal specifically with mathematics, have potential for older students' math learning. In Chapter 10 of Wilder's *Little House in the*

*Big Woods*, for example, Mary and Laura puzzle over how to share their two cookies with Baby Carrie so they each have a fair share. *Sadako and the Thousand Paper Cranes* (Coerr) is based on a true story of a Japanese girl who was sick but believed that if she folded one thousand paper cranes, the gods would grant her wish and make her well again. Not only does folding origami cranes support geometry learning, but students can also solve the problem of figuring out how long it would take to fold one thousand cranes.

Nonfiction books also spark ideas. The *Guinness Book of Records* and *50 Simple Things Kids Can Do to Save the Earth* (Earth Works Group) present an enormous amount of data that can engage students' thinking. Students can verify, for example, that "a leak that fills up a coffee cup in ten minutes will waste more than three thousand gallons of water in a year!" (Earth Works Group). Also, after reading "Smart," a poem from Silversteins's *Where the Sidewalk Ends*, students can check on how the boy exchanged a one dollar bill in various ways.

Don't count out integrating children's literature into math instruction for older students. There are dozens of options that can benefit your class.

| **Nine** | *The First* |
|---|---|
| | *Week* |
| | *of* |
| | *School* |

**K**yle *was facing the beginning of school as a first-year teacher. Amelia taught next door and was helping him get his room set up. In the math corner, they had put up some graphs, posted a problem to be solved, and arranged the manipulatives. "I'm really nervous about getting the year off on the right foot," Kyle said, "and I'm especially unsure of how to plunge in with math."*

*"I remember how terrified I was when I first started," Amelia answered and laughed. "At least you only have to live through your first day of teaching once. But it still takes me a lot of time to get ready for a new class. What's worrying you most?"*

*Kyle rattled off several questions. "What should I tell them about math? Is the activity I've planned for the first day a good idea? How do I find out what they know? How will I get them to handle using the materials?"*

*Kyle's first-day jitters are common to new and seasoned teachers alike. His concerns are real and valid. Much of the teaching you do throughout the year calls for responding to the particular needs of your students, and the first week is a critical and valuable foundation on which to build. So, what does this mean when you are thinking specifically about math instruction?*

## 71 How can I find out how my students feel about math, and why should I?

It's valuable to know how your students feel about mathematics. The more you know about your students in every way, the more effective you'll be as their teacher. In regard to their math learning, students who come to school comfortable with math are more likely to be eager to learn math lessons and patient when learning is challenging. They'll gobble up the lessons you offer. There are students, however, who find learning math difficult, or feel defeated by math. Knowing this is crucial for you so that you can begin to find ways to provide support and encouragement and help them discover their best learning styles.

So, how can you tell how your students feel about math? For most students, you can find out from their classroom participation and individual work. Pose problems for them to solve and pay attention to their reactions. Are they confident? Curious? Nervous? Eager? Reticent? Pose problems that are likely to engage students' interest and involvement, and watch how children react and respond. For example, try coin riddles with your class. They're useful problem-solving experiences that give children practice with calculating mentally. Put some coins in your pocket and think of clues. For young children just learning about the value of coins, an appropriate riddle might be: *I have two coins in my pocket worth 11 cents. What are they?* Ask children to raise a hand when they think they know the answer. See who is willing to respond and who isn't. Notice who needs to think, who seems to know easily, and who is baffled. After the children figure out the answer, show the coins to verify it. Then model how to count them, "A dime is worth 10 cents and a penny more makes 11 cents."

For a slightly more difficult task that's still appropriate for young children, give riddles for which there are more than one answer. For example: *I have six cents in my pocket. What coins could I have?* For this there are two possibilities: six pennies or a nickel and a penny. Give another clue. For example, if you had a nickel and a penny, your second clue might be one of these:

*I have exactly two coins.*

*I have fewer than five coins.*

*My coins aren't all the same kind.*

Again, notice how the children react.

For older students, use a larger amount of money for a more appropriate challenge—25 cents, for example. Give three clues, one at time. After each, ask the students what you might have in your pocket.

Clue 1: *I have fewer than 10 coins.*

Clue 2: *I have an even number of coins.*

Clue 3: *I have only two kinds of coins.*

The first clue produces seven possibilities, three with no pennies and three with five pennies. The second narrows the field to two choices: one dime and three nickels or one dime, two nickels, and five pennies. The third clue points to the answer of one dime and three nickels.

When posing these or other problems for your class to consider, it's useful to ask them from time to time, "Do you think this is too easy, too hard, or just right?" Tell the students that you'll say the words again, one at a time, and they're to listen and raise a hand for the one choice that best describes what they think. When doing this with young children, you may find that some raise a hand more than once or not at all. Make a note to talk with them later, and when you do, begin a conversation in the same way, asking, "Do you think the problem was too easy, too hard, or just right?" Then follow up with "What was easy (or hard) about it?"

Also, on written assignments, we've had success asking children to indicate at the bottom of a page whether the assignment was too easy, just right, or too hard. Sometimes, when we've prepared a worksheet or assignment, we write these on the bottom so students can indicate their reaction by checking a box:

❏ Too Easy ❏ Just Right ❏ Too Hard

Another way to find out about your students' attitudes, if you're teaching older children, is to frame some questions for them to discuss:

How would you describe yourself as a math student?

Where would you rank math in terms of subjects you enjoy more or less?

What can you describe about learning math in previous years?

What can you think of that's particularly hard about math?

What can you think of that's easy about math?

Lead a whole-class discussion, or perhaps even better, write the questions on the board and ask the students to huddle in small groups and share their thoughts and experiences. It's often safer for students to talk honestly in small groups and more students will have a chance to talk this way than in a whole-class discussion. Wander around and eavesdrop.

You'll probably hear both positive and negative tales. Some students will see math as a series of fun puzzles waiting to be solved, report having fun with math at home, or describe helping other classmates with math. Others will tell fright stories and recall embarrassing moments at the chalkboard, groan about difficult homework, or describe a sense of disillusionment. After students have had a chance to talk, you may want to ask them to write their math autobiographies so that you can read later about individuals' specific attitudes and experiences.

Any of these efforts will show your students that you're interested in how they feel about math. Be sure to thank them for the thoughts they share and tell them that they've given you valuable information that will help you teach them math this year. Assure them that one of your teaching goals is to help *all* students have a good year with math.

## 72 Okay, I have a sense of how my students feel about math. Now what should I communicate to my students about math?

Remember that how your students feel about mathematics when they begin school in September rests largely on their previous school experience and the tone at home. But how your students feel about mathematics when they leave your classroom relies on you. It's important for you to convey, through actions and words, that mathematics is essential in today's world. Show enthusiasm for math. Tell your students that you appreciate the usefulness of math. Reinforce for them that you value learning math. Of course if your own experience with learning math was difficult and these comments make you inwardly groan, don't try to fake an attitude of enthusiasm. Skip the commercial, try the next activity, and let it convey the message about the importance of math.

Lead a class discussion in which you ask students to think about how people use math in everyday life. You can prompt ideas by asking various questions:

What math ideas do you think about when figuring with time?

When do you need to add, subtract, multiply, or divide with numbers to find out something you need to know?

What math do you use when buying something from a store? using a recipe? sharing a snack?

List their ideas on the board or a sheet of chart paper. Title the list "Daily Math Activities" so you'll have visible verification that math skills are necessary for everyday life. And if you skipped the commercial before, try now to talk with your students about the value and importance of math in everyone's life.

Also, you might give older students the homework assignment of asking members of their families how they use math and then adding their contributions to the class list. The goal is for students to accept math as something that's important to their lives.

## 73 How can I find out what my students already understand?

Don't rely solely on the previous year's records. Some students may have spent the summer months internalizing all sorts of math concepts in practical, real-life situations. Other students may have lost ground in some of the concepts they only barely grasped during the previous year. Whatever their current understanding, remember that learning can be thought of as the journey that children make from simple awareness to robust understanding. As with any journey, there are fits and starts along the way, and part of your goal is for your students to gain robust understanding of the concepts you work with throughout the year and feel a sense of accomplishment.

Also, don't worry at this time about getting a complete handle on all the math that your students know. Focus on the specific math topic you'll be teaching first—subtraction, probability, circles, patterns, odd and even numbers, fractions, or whatever. Whether it's something that your students studied last year or a topic new to their math learning, have a beginning class discussion about what they know about the idea. Ask:

Who can tell something about _____?

What have you learned already about _____?

What are you interested in knowing about _____?

Another way to find out what students know is to give them a problem to solve. A mathematically rich problem is a way to begin collecting information about how your students think as well as what they can do and how far they can stretch within one particular situation. Let them know that the problem represents something they'll be learning about and that you're interested in what they know at this time. You might also tell them that sometime later you'll give them a similar problem and they'll have a chance to look at the progress they've made.

Choose a problem that students can solve using a variety of methods. To focus on addition, or counting by 10s, or thinking about multiplication as adding equal groups, you might ask first or second graders to figure out how many fingers there are in the class altogether. To focus on subtraction, give third or fourth graders the copyright date of the class dictionary or some other book and ask them to figure out the book's age. When starting to study comparing fractions, ask fifth graders to determine whether they've eaten more if they've had $\frac{5}{8}$ or $\frac{3}{4}$ of a pizza. Begin by asking volunteers to offer initial ideas about how they might figure out the answer. Then ask each child to record a solution and explain how he or she reached it. You'll learn about some children's thinking from the initial class discussion, and you'll learn about how individuals approach the problem from the written work. Assessing your children's abilities by having them explain their reasoning reveals much more than giving a traditional quiz and checking right answers does.

At the end of their work, use the suggestion we offered before (*see page 85*) and ask students to rank the difficulty of the problem—too easy, just right, or too hard. This not only gives you another useful indicator about students' comfort with a particular topic or problem, but also gives students the message that you're interested in how they feel about the assignment.

## 74 What classroom guidelines should I set up at the beginning of the year?

Your initial lessons in the year, along with giving you insights into what your students understand and how they approach math, should introduce the students to how they'll learn math throughout the year. Teacher's specific expectations and systems differ, but we recommend that in the first week's lessons you spend time with your class on four specifics aspects of instruction—the topics students will study, how students will be organized for learning, the materials they'll use, and how they'll be expected to engage in and communicate about their math learning.

The math topics first: It's valuable for students to understand the range of math they'll study. You might use the national content standards for this or the areas of mathematics identified by your district or state. Post a chart of the math topics you'll cover. We're big on posting charts so that there are visual reminders in the classroom of things you think are important. For example, a chart might list the following:

Number

Geometry

Measurement

Statistics

Probability

Algebra

In the first week, establish the routine of referring to the list when introducing lessons and identifying the area or areas that the day's lesson concentrates on. All of the assessment suggestions offered in the previous section, for example, focused on number. Be sure to introduce lessons during the first week that include other topics as well.

To focus on how students will be organized for learning, provide opportunities during the first week for students to participate in whole-class lessons, work in pairs or small groups, and complete individual assignments. Think about how you expect students to engage in each different situation. Tell them, for example, that in whole-class lessons only one person talks at a time and everyone else should listen to what's being said. When working with partners or in small groups, lots of children will be talking at the same time, so it's important for them to keep their voices down. And there will be times when you'll ask them to do individual work and not talk with their classmates. Communicate your guidelines and give students the chance to put them into action. Discuss and reinforce the guidelines regularly.

Introduce students to the materials they'll be using regularly throughout the year—paper, measuring tools, manipulatives, calculators, and so on. Establish procedures for their use, such as whether they're available at all times or only at times you designate. Show the students where each material is stored and be clear that they're to be responsible when using them. (*See pages 53–54 for specific guidelines about using manipulatives.*)

Finally, establish from the beginning how you expect students to engage as math learners. For example, it may be new to some students that they are expected to get actively involved in lessons, to think and reason, and to communicate about their math learning orally in whole-class and small-group discussions and also in written assignments. Spend time at the beginning of the year giving the students experience with participating actively and communicating. Reinforce your guidelines regularly. The attention you give will help you and your students enjoy a productive year of math learning.

## 75 Can you recommend favorite lessons for the beginning of the year that help establish and reinforce classroom guidelines?

A disclaimer first: The danger of identifying favorite lessons is that what seems interesting as we write may appear stale and have long been replaced by the time you read it. That said, a candidate for the favorite category is to build math lessons around something that has a direct connection to students—their names. Not only do name activities offer a personal perspective for doing math and help classmates learn one another's names, but they have several other beneficial attributes. They can involve students with two important math topics (number and statistics), several different classroom organizations (whole-class, small-group, individual), and a manipulative material (interlocking cubes). Also, the ideas are adaptable to different grade levels, lend themselves to homework assignments, model how to engage students in thinking and reasoning, and introduce how a lesson can extend beyond one math period to last for several days.

If you like the idea of using students' names for math investigations, begin by giving students three-by-three-inch Post-it Notes on which they write their first names. Have students come to the board one by one and post their names, organizing the Post-it Notes into a graph by placing names with the same number of letters in the same row. Discuss the graph:

What's the range of numbers of letters used for our first names?

Which number of letters occurs most often? How many more students have five-letter names than two-letter names?

How many fewer students have six-letter names than three-letter names?

Then, depending on the grade level, follow this introductory activity with one or more of the following ideas.

**1. Ask first and second graders to make trains with interlocking cubes to represent their first names, using one cube for each letter.**

Ask two children with different length first names, for example, Tom and Janet, to come to the front of the room with their trains. Pose questions, discuss, and record results:

Which has more letters? (Record: 5 > 3)

How many more letters are there in Janet's name? (Record: 3 + 2 = 5 or 5 − 3 = 2)

Which has fewer letters? (Record: 3 < 5)

How many letters are there in your names altogether? (Record: 3 + 5 = 8)

Assign pairs of children with different length first names. Ask them to write their names on a sheet of paper, then compare their trains and write as many math sentences as they can.

**2. Ask second, third, or fourth graders to make another graph, this time for their last names.**

Discuss how the two graphs are the same and how they differ. Pose the problem: *Does our class use more letters for our last names than our first names?* Ask children to make predictions. Then have them work in pairs to find out. Ask them to write about how they reached their conclusion. Collect their papers. For homework, ask children to check their local telephone book and figure out how many people have the same last name as theirs and bring the information to class. The next day, discuss what they learned from the telephone book investigation and also discuss their solutions about the last name problem.

**3. Ask older students to think about the average length of their first names.**

Introduce the idea of *mode* by looking at which name length occurs most often. Introduce the idea of *median* by having students line up in order of name length and seeing how long the name is of the student who lands in the middle of the line. For the *mean*, ask students to make trains of interlocking cubes using one cube for each letter in their first names. Have them either give away cubes or get some from other students to try to "even out" the trains so that each student's train is the same length or almost the same length. Then do the calculation by adding the number of letters in each name and dividing by the number of students. Compare the results from the trains and from the calculation. (*See page 13 for another suggestion for teaching students about mean, median, and mode.*)

## 76 Should I communicate with parents right away? If so, what should I say?

One of the best investments you can make during the first week or two of school is to touch base with the parents of each child in your class. Call parents at home in the late afternoon, early evening, or over the weekend. Introduce yourself as their child's teacher and say that you're delighted to have their child in your class. Next, explain that you are calling the parents of each child and asking if there is anything they'd like to tell you about their child.

Then get your pencils ready. Parents, for the most part, will be more than happy to address your query with a thorough response. You'll hear everything from the student's relationship with neighborhood children to his or her extraordinary talent in building with Legos. Parents may also tell you about familial and/or health issues, such as a pending divorce, an illness in the family, or food allergies. Mostly listen and take copious notes. After all, it's too early for you to have formed a solid impression of this child—and certainly too early for you to have made a firm judgment of any kind.

You might wish to ask parents about their early school careers—which content areas they particularly enjoyed. It's useful for you to know about parents who readily convey a strong favor or disfavor of mathematics. Children learn what they live, and if you plan to make eager math learners of all of your students, you may need to reach their parents as well. (*See page 14 for other thoughts about children who dislike math.*) At the end of the conversation, you should have a much clearer, broader picture of the student with whom you will spend thirty hours a week for the next ten months. Thank parents for their time and remind them of your commitment to their child's success.

One more bonus: At some point down the road, you may need to speak with one of your student's parents again regarding an academic or behavioral issue. But it won't be the first interaction with the parents. You've already established that you have the child's best interests at heart and that you didn't prejudge him or her. Therefore, the chances of you being able to work in concert with the parents for the benefit of the child are much greater because of the groundwork you laid in September. Enlist parents as your allies right away. It pays off again and again throughout the year and enables you to teach the students in your class more effectively.

We realize that calling parents is an enormous commitment. Yes, we know that it takes a lot of time to make these calls and have these conversations. But the effort is worth it. It's time and energy well spent for what it contributes to building a partnership with parents for supporting their child's learning.

|         | Connecting |
|---------|-----------|
| **Ten** | *with*     |
|         | *Parents*  |

The annual fall back-to-school night was coming up. Carrie was thinking about how best to present her math program to the parents so that they would have a sense of how the children were learning math and how families could support that learning at home. She wondered, "How can I assure parents that their children are learning the basics but also give them a feel for the excitement I'm trying to build with math? What handouts could I prepare that would help them understand the math program and what they can expect?"

Carrie was thinking about an activity that would involve the parents and give them firsthand experience with the way their children were learning math. And then she remembered the "new math" question from last year. A parent expressed that he had been scarred by new math when he was in school and wanted to be sure it wouldn't happen to his daughter. Her thoughts shifted to planning how to respond to this issue if it were to come up again.

Careful planning for connecting with parents is essential, whether it's at back-to-school night, during parent conferences, or through some other teacher-parent interaction. The more advance thinking and planning you do, the better prepared you'll be.

## 77 How should I prepare for back-to-school night?

Back-to-school night presents an opportunity for you to show parents how you will impact their children's lives throughout the school year. At back-to-school night, parents will evaluate your capability for teaching math, your classroom organization, and your teaching demeanor. With thought and planning, you can make parents leave your classroom with the confidence that their child will have a successful year.

Let's begin with your capability. Giving parents a personal glimpse into your program will build their understanding of the math instruction you're offering their child. And building their understanding is the best way to build their confidence. Begin with a hands-on, minds-on activity that you've already done with the class. You might choose to introduce an activity with a manipulative material to help parents experience how you're making abstract math ideas concrete for their children. If you teach young children, ask parents to build several trains ten cubes long using only two colors of interlocking cubes. Connect their trains to addition equations, pointing out how this is a way for children to explore different addition combinations and learn the correct mathematical symbolism to represent them. If you teach older students, ask parents to build different size rectangles using twelve color tiles and point out how this helps model multiplication. Or give them Cuisenaire rods, ask them to find pairs of rods in which one is half the length of the other, and then talk about how this will help their children learn about fractions. *(See Figure 10–1.)*

Whatever material you choose, relate it to some math concept that parents are familiar with so they can see how the materials would have helped them when they were children. In this way, parents can become enthusiastic supporters of using materials.

If you prefer not to introduce manipulatives, post a few charts and graphs on which parents can record data about themselves as they arrive. If possible, select

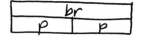
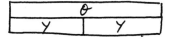

**10–1.** Parents get firsthand experience with how their children begin to learn fractions by finding pairs of Cuisenaire rods.

some that your class has already worked with so that you can show parents their children's versions later. You might want to try some of the name graphs we suggested earlier. *(See page 89.)* Or you might draw a large Venn diagram with three intersecting circles. Title the diagram "Pets at Home." Label the circles "We have a dog." "We have a cat." "We have fish." *(See Figure 10–2.)* Ask parents to mark one "X" to indicate their pet profile.

Another idea is an estimation activity. Fill a jar with three scoops of rice or beans, set the jar and scoop on a table, and post a large grid made from ruling squares on chart paper. Also post directions that ask parents to estimate the number of scoops the jar will hold when it's full and then color in a square in the correct column to indicate their estimates. Write numbers across the bottom that are reasonable estimates for the jar you chose. Or ask parents to figure out the "value" of their first name, using a = 1¢, b = 2¢, c = 3¢, and so on. List values on a chart and post directions for parents to put a tally mark to indicate their name's value.

Or choose some other activity that your students have done and ask the parents to try it. Save your children's work from the same activity so you can distribute it to their parents later in the evening. Parents will really enjoy seeing their children's version of an activity they've experienced. To conclude, present a chart you've prepared that lists the concepts you plan to introduce during the course of the year to give parents a look at the overall curriculum. Talk about the sequence of topics that the children will be learning and show the parents the instructional materials that you'll use during the year.

Now it's time to reveal your organizational skills. Explain how the children will work during math time—sometimes in pairs or small groups, sometimes as a whole

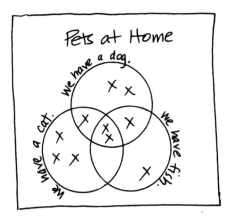

**10–2.** Parents use a Venn diagram to indicate their personal pet profiles.

class, and at times independently. Stress that regardless of how children work, they will be expected to explain their thinking and justify their responses. Explain that lessons vary in length, lasting for part of a class period or stretching over several days, depending on the nature, scope, and value of the lesson. Reinforce that once students study a concept in your class, they are expected to apply it again and again in different settings. Take a moment to show parents where the manipulative materials and other supplies are kept. If you haven't introduced them before, you may want to display and identify samples of the manipulatives you'll use often and explain their purpose. *(For help with this, see page 52.)* Inform parents about the sort of work they can expect their child to bring home, and give any other information that you think will help them get a feel for how you run the class. And emphasize that you are always looking for mathematically sound thinking, not just right answers, that your goal is for the children to become independent, creative, and critical thinkers who enjoy math and are eager learners.

The issue of your demeanor is easy. Greet parents with a smile and warmly welcome them into your classroom. This, along with being well prepared for the evening, sends an important message. Parents will feel that any teacher who makes such a clear, thorough, and personal presentation must be caring and capable.

## 78 Should I prepare handouts to give parents on back-to-school night? If so, what should they be?

We have three suggestions for handouts: an overview of the year's curriculum, guidelines for questions that support children's math learning, and a glossary of math terms that the children will be learning and using during the year. Consider preparing one or more of these.

For an overview of the year's curriculum, the easiest solution is to duplicate an excerpt of your district math framework, standards, or course of study so that parents can read about the expectations for your grade level. Talk about topics that they may not be familiar with or recall from their own math learning. Also, refer to the list you posted earlier *(see page 94)* and explain a bit about the instructional materials you use.

Give parents guidelines for questions that support math learning. Prepare a list of the kinds of questions that you'll be asking routinely during math class, and take a moment to elaborate on each of them. Tell parents that asking questions like "How many are left?" and "What's the answer?" aren't enough to assess what children understand. Questions or prompts such as "How did you find your answer?" "Tell me more about what you did." "How can you be sure that your answer makes sense?" and "Is there another way to solve the problem?" reveal more about how a child is thinking. If children can answer these questions, parents can be confident that they will be successful in answering any and all of the simpler "How many are left?" type questions. As you review your list of questions with parents, suggest that they use these types of questions when reviewing papers that children bring home or helping their child with homework.

Provide parents with a glossary of math terms that children will be learning throughout the course of the year. You might find such a list in the back of your instructional materials or in your district course of study. Many parents will benefit from having at their fingertips definitions for familiar terms such as *addend, sum, difference, product, dividend, divisor, multiple, factor, equivalent,* and so forth. While parents know many of these terms, they may appreciate a refresher. How many terms should the glossary contain? That depends on the terminology you expect your students to understand and use as they communicate with one another about math during class.

## 79 I know some of my students' parents dislike math. What advice can I give them so they don't pass their attitude on to their children?

It's possible that one or more of your students' parents will come up to you during back-to-school night and say something like, "You know, I always did poorly in math. Never liked it. Seems like Johnny is just a chip off the old block!" You probably won't be able to change these parents' attitudes, but you can and should help them see what they can do to ensure against their children embracing the same negative attitude. Offer them the following three suggestions.

Begin by being direct and asking parents not to pass on their negative attitude to their child. Parents have a great deal to do with children's attitudes—about everything. You've heard the adage "Children learn what they live." It's true. Especially for young children, parents are the leading authorities on everything, from school to food and everything in between. Parents should avoid talking about math in a negative way or revealing to their child that they did poorly in math. It simply doesn't help their child. Instead, parents should display an attitude of curiosity toward the math their child is learning.

Next, ask parents to let their child see and hear them do math as it comes up during the day. There are many, many opportunities for this—balancing the checkbook, measuring the amount of wallpaper needed for the bathroom, mixing fertilizer for the lawn, figuring out savings after a discount is taken, keeping score when playing a game, and on and on. In these sorts of situations, parents should let their child in on their thinking. They can count out loud when digging in a pocket for change at the cash register, for example, or talk about how they're measuring $\frac{2}{3}$ of a cup of broth. And they should offer their thinking without grumbling or showing any negativity!

Third, ask parents to involve their child in doing math. Most parents have enjoyed the closeness of cuddling up and reading with their children. Ask them to imagine the same sort of closeness with doing math. Ask them to let their child help with math figuring that's needed—calculating change or figuring the time the family needs to leave to get to Grandma's on time, for example. Doing so will be enormously beneficial to their child's mathematical future. Not only will following these suggestions benefit children, but it may also help make progress toward changing parents' poor attitudes. Hating math is learned; it can be unlearned.

## 80 Parents want to know how they can help their children, but some are afraid that they won't know how or will do the wrong thing. How can I address this at back-to-school night?

Some parents say that their child is learning math in ways that are foreign to them. Other parents have reported that when they've shown their child the way they learned to do something, their child comes home saying that it was the wrong way. "The teacher says I have to do it like this," we've heard children report. In general, some parents aren't sure if they should help their child, and they're sometimes not sure if they can.

It's true that some of the ways we teach math today won't be familiar to parents. This can make parents feel intimidated about helping. Also, we know that parents who are trying to help sometimes show their child how to do something that the child can repeat by rote but doesn't really understand. Still, the parents are trying to help and it's important not to demean the effort.

For example, Sophie, a first grader, came to school and proudly announced to the teacher, "I know how to borrow." She showed what she meant, writing a three-digit subtraction problem that required regrouping and then solving it correctly, impressive for a first grader. The teacher acknowledged that the answer was correct and Sophie beamed, proud of her new learning. However, when the teacher wrote a problem horizontally, $350 - 150$, Sophie was stumped. Then she brightened. "I can do it," she said. She rewrote the problem with 150 underneath the 350, and proceeded methodically to subtract from right to left as her mother had shown her, focused on the procedure rather than on the quantities.

David's father was a physicist. To help David learn to add fractions, he showed him a shortcut that worked for all problems. David was eager to show his teacher. For $\frac{2}{3} + \frac{3}{5}$, he demonstrated how he "cross-multiplied" (2 times 5 and then 3 times 3) and added the two products (10 plus 9 is 19). "That's the top of the answer," David said. Then David multiplied the denominators (3 times 5). "And that's the new bottom number," he said. David also knew that the answer of $\frac{19}{15}$ was the same as $1\frac{4}{15}$.

Think about how you would respond to students in situations like these. One thing we advise *not* to say to a student is, "We don't do it that way in our class." You don't want to make parents feel uncomfortable or that they're interfering and cause them to pull back from being involved in their child's learning. You want parents to share their knowledge and understanding. Take the positive road. Let your students know that there are many different ways to arrive at solutions, but also tell them that it's important in their math learning for them to be able to explain why something works. Don't disparage their contribution, but work with them to figure out why it makes sense. For Sophie, that meant getting her to think about the quantities, not merely the procedure. Just as we don't want children dependent on calculators for simple computations, we don't want them dependent on paper and pencil for computations they can—and should—do mentally. In David's case, the teacher had never seen this method and told David so. The teacher said, "Thanks for showing it to me. I need to think about why it works, and then we'll talk more about it."

## 81 My students' parents are mostly concerned about the basics. How should I address this concern?

When they mention basics, most parents are talking about arithmetic skills, which often is the only math topic they remember being taught when they were in school. And most of what they remember is doing pages of computation practice, perhaps coupled with solving word problems. Today's curriculum, however, takes a broader look at arithmetic. Parents need information about this shift, and they also need reassurance about the importance of arithmetic in your math program and how their children will be helped to learn the basics.

Following are ways to address these issues. We've written them as letters to parents so that if you don't want to address this issue during back-to-school night, you can send information home at another time. Feel free to change the letters, personalize them, and use them in any way that helps you communicate with your students' families.

Here's a letter about arithmetic in general:

Dear Parent,

As when you were in elementary school, arithmetic is still the major emphasis of your child's math learning. However, today's arithmetic program has three important areas: computation, problem solving, and number sense. The goals are for children to learn to compute accurately and efficiently; apply skills to solve problems; and develop the numerical intuition needed to reason flexibly, make reasonable estimates, and judge whether answers make sense. Here are some ways you can support your child's learning at home:

- Empty your pocket or change purse each evening and have your child count how much money there is.
- Have your child figure change when you're shopping.
- Ask for help figuring out what time to leave in order to get somewhere on time.
- Play games that involve doing arithmetic.
- When you fill your gas tank, ask an older child to figure the gas mileage.

The more number activities you do that you and your child can enjoy together, the more help you'll be providing.

And one specifically about computation:

Dear Parent,

Most of us equate learning math in elementary school with the many pages of arithmetic drill we did when we were students. While it's important for students to learn to compute accurately and efficiently, computational proficiency on paper-and-pencil exercises is no longer the acceptable minimum standard for arithmetic competency. Basic arithmetic skills are broader and reflect more rigor, preparing students not only to develop skills but also to learn to apply them in new, different, and more complex situations. Students today must be able to

- identify which operations to use when solving problems;
- choose the numbers to use;
- do the calculations—either mentally, with paper and pencil, or using a calculator; and
- evaluate the reasonableness of the answer and decide what to do if it isn't reasonable.

Our goal in school is not only for children to learn to compute correct answers but also for them to be able to explain how they did so and to learn to apply the skill to problem-solving situations. When your child brings work home, ask questions that give you insights into what your child understands: "Can you explain how you figured?" "How do you know the answer makes sense?" "Do you know another way to do it?"

## 82 What should I tell parents about math homework?

Parents will want to know about homework, since it's the main source of communication between you, the child, and them. (*See Chapter 11, "Handling Homework."*) Offer a broad view of what you expect to accomplish through homework. Make sure you impress upon parents the purposes of homework: to reinforce, apply, or extend the learning that's going on in your classroom.

Parents may ask you how often you'll assign homework and the nature of the assignments. Your school or district may have a policy that requires you to assign a certain amount of homework, or it may be up to you how often you'll assign homework. Either way, it's important that you have a ready answer.

In regard to the nature of assignments, tell parents that assignments will vary, depending on the purpose and nature of your work in the classroom. During a measurement unit, you might ask children to estimate the area of their kitchen floor or find items that weigh about a pound. That's quite different from an assignment asking children to practice a procedure they've learned for finding products or quotients.

Parents may ask you how much they should help their child with homework. Again, it depends on the assignment. Explain that it's perfectly fine for the whole family to be involved in the discussion relating to estimating the area of a kitchen. But an assignment designed to reinforce a procedure that has been explored and studied in class is meant to be largely independent. Tell parents to notify you when their child needs extensive help on an assignment that appears to be designed for the child to complete independently.

## 83 A colleague told me that parents sometimes ask about "new math" and the question often brings snickers from others. What do they mean by "new math" and how should I respond to such questions?

A short history lesson can help with this. The first half of the 1960s was the time of "new math," a movement sparked by the Russian launching of Sputnik in 1957. The Russians were ahead in the space race and there was widespread support across the country to change how we were teaching math so that we could keep up. "New math" was created, pushing school mathematics beyond arithmetic. Teachers were now to guide students to discover abstract mathematical principles through the process of deduction. But "new math" caused mass confusion among teachers and parents alike, and the plan backfired. Only university mathematicians seemed happy. What was the problem? While expanding the content of the math curriculum made sense, one miscalculation of "new math" was teacher preparedness. The new expanded content covered areas of mathematics unfamiliar to many teachers, especially those who taught the early grades. Teachers valiantly tried teaching about sets and number bases from the new texts, but it wasn't successful. Remember, you can't teach what you don't really understand.

In the 1970s, "new math" fell on hard times and the math education pendulum swung toward a "back to the basics" movement that now swept the nation. Teachers were to return to age-old tried-and-true arithmetic teaching. We were to go back to the good old days—as if there really had been good old days. There hadn't. In the early 1950s, two-thirds of United States high school students ended their math career after the freshman year.

A disturbing situation emerged in the 1980s, following the "back to the basics" movement. National assessments showed that while students were learning the arithmetic skills of addition, subtraction, multiplication, and division, they couldn't apply these skills to solve problems. Students' inability to reason seemed to indicate that they really didn't understand why they were pushing numbers here and there. The following test item from the 1982 National Assessment of Educational Progress illustrates the problem:

Estimate the answer to $\frac{12}{13} + \frac{7}{8}$ .

    a. 1

    b. 2

    c. 19

    d. 21

Among thirteen-year-olds, approximately equal numbers of students chose each answer, with 24 percent making the correct choice. Of the seventeen-year-olds, only 37 percent made the correct choice!

Many educators took notice of the situation and various organizations, including the National Council of Teachers of Mathematics and the Mathematical Sciences Education Board, got on board to improve the teaching of mathematics. The Committee on the Mathematical Sciences in the Year 2000 was established, and the math education pendulum reversed its direction. Problem solving became the emphasis of instruction through the 1980s.

One problem with a swinging educational pendulum is that people tend to line up on one side or the other. However, in classrooms, teachers still strive for doing what's best for the students, drawing from all the resources available. The 1990s were a time in which standards were introduced to try to pull all that we had learned about effective math teaching into a coherent and cohesive whole. National math standards were first introduced in March 1989; many states used these as guidelines for their own math standards and new assessments; and then the national standards were revised and released in April 2000. (*See page 2 for information about the current standards.*)

Education will always be a work in progress. Changes will always occur, both in and out of schools, that require us to rethink what we're doing and how we're meeting the needs of the children we're schooling. Technology, for example, has given one of the biggest pushes to our lives in general, and as a result, to education. Even though the future is always unpredictable, we still have to consider it as best we can when making teaching decisions and communicating with parents about the choices we make.

## 84 How much math work should I send home?

Sending home work done in math class is a way to communicate with parents about what their child is doing in math. The quick answer is to send home enough so that parents can see the kind of work their child is doing and will be reassured about their child's math learning. Your school may have a policy about how much to send; it seems that at least once a week makes sense. Be sure that work you send home reflects what a child knows, just as work you save should provide insights into children's thinking and learning.

The answer of "how much" doesn't address a much more important issue, however. What involvement would you like parents to have with their child's math work? Do you want a response from them? If so, what sort of feedback would you like? Again, we don't have a particular strategy to recommend. Communication with parents is important, and your decision in this regard should relate to the thinking you do about the importance you put on homework, report cards, and parent conferences.

## 85 Parent conferences are coming. What should I have ready?

The best materials to have ready for a parent conference are samples of the child's work. While giving parents information about their child's math progress is important, the child's actual papers will bring to life the information you're offering and help make it concrete. (*See page 69 for information about collecting student work.*) You may want to present a child's work chronologically, celebrating with parents the growth their child has exhibited and talking about the needs you're addressing. Or you may prefer to choose a few work samples to talk about that illustrate specific points—a child's special math triumph, an area of weakness, or a skill learned well, for example.

Review each paper that you plan to share with parents ahead of time so that you know what you want to point out to parents. Think about what the sample communicates to parents. You might jot notes on a Post-it to jog your memory when the parents are in front of you. Not only will this planning help your conversation with parents during the conference, but it's also an opportunity for you to focus on each of your students' progress, strengths, and needs.

## 86 How can I begin a parent conference? Should I ask parents what questions they have?

Before you invite parents to ask you the questions that are on their minds, try to get a sense of their view. How do they think their child is doing in math? Do they see their child struggling with homework assignments? Does their child ask questions that reflect an interest in math? Asking parents questions like these can help broaden your view of the child and also give you information about parents' concerns.

However, you should be prepared to respond to the question typically on parents' minds: "How is my child doing in math at school?" Here is where you'll share with parents the papers you've collected and reviewed ahead of time. Go through one work sample at a time, highlighting what you recall from rereading your Post-it Notes. Don't worry about parents seeing your Post-it Notes; they'll appreciate that you took additional time to prepare for their visit. You may also want to offer an anecdote that captures a particular child for his or her parents. Perhaps it will be an insightful comment that the child made during an exploration. Maybe you can recall a time when the child persuaded other students that his or her estimate was reasonable or that a procedure he or she used was the most efficient. In any case, parents will enjoy hearing something that sets their child apart from the others and that makes them realize that you've paid attention to and know about their child.

Parents may ask you some questions that you can't answer immediately off the top of your head. Fine! Don't try to invent an answer on the spot. Tell the parents that you need additional time to think about a response. Then do the research required and get back to them as soon as possible.

## 87 What should I say if parents want to know how they can help their child in math?

Some parents will ask this. Your answer, of course, depends on the child. In some instances, you may feel a child is doing fine in math but have a specific suggestion to offer the parents that could enhance the child's learning. Some students, for example, might benefit from help with developing their number sense, and you can show parents a few simple math games that would be useful. Card games and dominoes are two familiar options. Some children are strong readers and are more interested in books than in math, and you might suggest some children's books that could help build the child's interest in math. (*See Chapter 8 for ideas about connecting math and children's literature.*) Some children might need help at home memorizing the addition or times table. (*See pages 43–45 for suggestions with this.*)

If you have serious concerns about the math progress of any of the children in your class, be clear and honest with parents. These children would most likely benefit from additional one-on-one attention, and the best approach might be to enlist a parent's help.

Even when children are doing fine and you don't have a specific suggestion, you can still help parents think about how to support their child's math learning. Most importantly, parents should be helping their child see math as integral and useful to his or her life and as a subject worth studying. Caution parents not to confine their math experiences at home to dining room table torture, but to involve their child with math as often as possible in the course of daily events. If you want to offer parents just one tip in this light, suggest that they think aloud each time they use math themselves—making change at the store, arranging the carpool schedule, calculating the time needed for the turkey to roast, or figuring out the wages for the babysitter. Getting parents in the habit of doing this helps lift math off the pages of school assignments and relates it to real-world needs. It's a valuable and far-reaching strategy.

# Eleven | *Handling Homework*

*F*elicia felt that she was providing her children with a rich math experience in her classroom. "Do I have to give homework?" she thought. "In class, I'm able to monitor what they're doing and I can stay on top of their learning. I can't do that with homework assignments. Besides, homework just means I have more papers to read and grade. Assigning homework drags me down, and it's too time-consuming for the children and for me."

*Jane felt differently. It seemed she never had enough time to spend on math during school hours. "Well," she thought, "we'll just get started with this lesson now and I'll let the students finish it at home. Then I can pick up tomorrow and keep moving along."*

*Why do you assign homework? What sorts of homework assignments can support learning? What should you do with the assignments the children complete? And what can you do about students who don't do their homework? It's important to think about the role of homework in your math instruction and also how to communicate the role of homework to parents.*

## 88 What are the purposes of math homework?

Homework can serve several purposes. It can be used to reinforce, apply, or extend the math children are learning in class. You can assign practice, provide experience with solving problems, or ask children to gather data that you'll use in the next day's lesson. Also, homework is a useful vehicle for students to communicate with their families about what they're learning in school. You may ask children to show their parents a game they played in class, talk with them about a problem they solved recently, or share a newly learned skill. Assignments like these give children the opportunity to teach their parents something they've learned. They also give the child the chance to be an expert at home, while parents learn more about their child's math program.

As with lessons, there's no single right or best way to think about homework. A variety of assignments will certainly be most effective. Also, be sure you've gauged the complexity of an assignment before you give it to decide whether it's reasonable. If you're assigning a problem to be solved, for example, it's important that you've tried it yourself. If the assignment calls for gathering data, make sure it's doable for your students. You don't want homework to pose unnecessary difficulties for your students or their families.

## 89 What options are there for dealing with homework that the children did the night before?

You may remember your teachers collecting your homework, correcting it, and returning it to you in a day or two. Reading each student's work gives teachers information in two ways: it provides a general class response to what they've been teaching and specific information about individual students. While this sort of information is useful to you, your feedback is only useful to students if they have the opportunity to reflect on what they did. Other ways of following up on homework assignments may give students more effective feedback.

One way that has worked well for us is to begin class by having students share their homework in pairs or small groups. Their task is to compare results and, if there are different answers, try to figure out what's right. For some homework assignments, however, there are several possible correct answers. In these cases, students need to check that one another's answers make sense. In all situations, keep the focus on understanding the assignment and learning, not merely on getting right or wrong answers.

It's typical in most classes that some students won't complete an assignment. But when this situation comes up, it's good for students who didn't do an assignment at least to have the opportunity to talk with others. This keeps them involved in the learning, which is the main goal of assigning homework in the first place. For everyone in a group to agree on the results, some students may have to work a bit harder to include someone who didn't complete the assignment. But doing so can reinforce their learning as well.

It helps if you have an efficient system for checking that students have completed homework assignments. If you collect them, it's easy to do later. If students are comparing assignments in groups, however, go quickly around the room and check. Then circulate and listen as groups work.

You may also want to pose a follow-up problem based on the homework for groups to tackle. For example, first graders studying about money prepared in class for a homework assignment by folding an $8\frac{1}{2}$-by-14-inch sheet of paper in half and half again, both the short way, to make four columns. They did a coin rubbing at the top of each column, using a penny, a nickel, a dime, and a quarter. (*See Figure 11–1.*)

Their assignment was to find something at home that cost each amount, and then draw, describe, and/or paste it on the paper under the appropriate coin. The teacher duplicated directions and sent them home so that parents knew how to help. The next day, children worked in pairs, first comparing their purchases and then figuring out how much they would each spend if they bought something with each coin, how much the two of them would spend, and how much they thought the entire class would spend.

Fifth graders learning about area and perimeter had the homework assignment of drawing three shapes, each with a perimeter of 30 centimeters. They had to draw their shapes on centimeter-squared paper following two guidelines: draw only on the lines and draw a shape that will remain in one piece if you cut it out of the paper. (*See Figure 11–2.*)

The students' shapes differed, and group members had the task of checking one another's shapes to be sure the perimeters were correct. Then the teacher gave a follow-up assignment for them to cut out two of their group's figures, the one with the largest area and the one with the smallest, and post them on a class chart. The teacher talked with the class about how the shapes with larger and smaller areas differed.

After pairs or groups confer, initiate a class discussion both about the content of

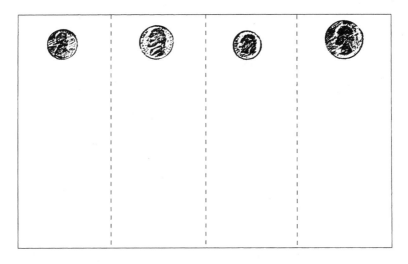

**11–1.** First graders prepare their homework paper for an assignment about money.

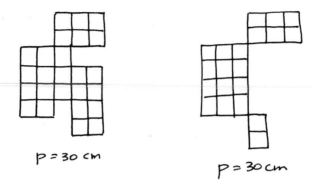

OK

not OK

p = 30 cm

p = 30 cm

**11–2.** For homeowrk, students draw shapes that have a perimeter of 30 centimeters on centimeter-squared paper. In class, they'll compare the areas of the shapes they drew.

the assignment and about their group work. Questions for this discussion might include: "Who would like to report the results? Who can report something you learned from a groupmate? If you disagreed about an answer, how did you resolve it? Who changed his or her mind about an answer? What helped you to do so?"

An important note: It's imperative that children understand the purpose of their homework. Students need to feel that you're asking them to spend their time on something that's of value. They also need to see the connection the assignment has to their classroom learning. The homework you assign must make sense to children.

## 90 What should I do about children who don't do their math homework?

There most likely will be times during the course of the year when some children do not complete their math homework. Each case is different and requires a slightly different treatment on your part as the teacher. When a child neglects to return homework once in a great while, it's probably a minor issue that you can address lightly. However, if and when a child neglects to do or return homework on a regular basis, it may be an indication of a larger issue that you need to address. If this is the case, you should do so swiftly and tactfully.

You may find that on the same day, several children neglect to turn in their homework. That may indicate that the assignment you gave wasn't clear or was too difficult, given the knowledge they currently have on the topic. Either way, address the situation immediately with the class. Encourage an open forum, so that you can ascertain what went wrong. If the directions were unclear to your students, perhaps a simple clarification is all they need before giving it another try. Perhaps, after some reflection, you will decide that the assignment you gave is more suitable for class work under your supervision. The other possibility is that the homework assignment wasn't appropriate for students to tackle on their own. You may want to devote class time to it or, perhaps, revise it in some way and give it a try as another assignment.

### 91 What should I tell parents about helping their children with homework assignments?

Should parents help with homework assignments? Generally, the amount of parent involvement you want or need depends on the assignment you give. If the assignment is one that reinforces something that the children have learned, then parents shouldn't need to help. But if the assignment is one that extends their learning, perhaps a problem-solving application of something students learned in class, parents' assistance may be preferred. And if the assignment is a data-collecting or information-gathering activity, it may be more effective if the parents are involved. So the nature of the assignment will dictate whether you anticipate parent involvement.

Let's say your homework assignment for a given day involves reinforcing something you believe that children understand well. They may be practicing a skill that has been explored and discussed in small groups, with partners, or as a class. They may have completed some similar work by themselves in the classroom. In your mind, this is largely an independent assignment that you expect children to complete on their own. There will be children who ask their parents for help or support. Some may simply want a parent to read the directions to them. Or they may want their parents to sit beside them for the duration of the assignment. Some parents, in the spirit of being helpful and involved, actually do their child's thinking and/or recording. A child who habitually makes math homework a family affair needs your attention.

Of course, if a child experiences a great deal of difficulty completing a specific assignment, you want parents to alleviate their child's stress and perhaps assist with the completion of the assignment. But if that's the case, you need to know it. Urge parents to jot a note explaining what transpired during the completion of the homework assignment. Then speak with the child privately at some time during the day. You may ask the child some questions about the homework itself, as well as questions about the math he or she needs to know in order to complete it independently. If clarification is needed, offer it immediately. If the child understands the math required to complete the homework successfully, then encourage him or her to tackle future assignments of a similar nature independently.

At times you might give an assignment that's a data-collecting or information-gathering activity. Let's say you want children to record the number of times the telephone rings from the time they get home from school until their bedtimes. Perhaps the same day, a child has an early evening activity or wants to play outside with some friends. In this case, it's perfectly appropriate for the family to chip in and continue the record keeping. You want information from every child in the class, if at all possible. Since the purpose of the assignment is to gather data for use in a future activity, it's not necessarily reflective of what children know and can do.

The way in which children complete their homework often reflects their confidence as learners and thinkers. You, as the teacher, must create an atmosphere accepting enough so that children feel they can approach you with pride or with frustration and anxiety. And you must strive to communicate to parents that they can confide in you with concerns about their child's attitude and performance during homework time.

<table>
<tr><td rowspan="4" align="center">**Twelve**</td><td>*Preparing*</td></tr>
<tr><td>*for*</td></tr>
<tr><td>*Administrator*</td></tr>
<tr><td>*Observations*</td></tr>
</table>

**N**ick *was new to the school this year and was also new to teaching third grade. He was talking with Sam about getting ready for being observed by Justine, the principal.*

*"We're kind of in the middle of a unit," he told Sam, "and the kids are all involved in different projects. I'm not sure a lesson like this really shows how the students are learning. I'm nervous."*

*"If you're not sure, you can take a break from the unit and do a lesson that's related but more self-contained," Sam advised.*

*Nick had other questions as well. "How much should I involve manipulatives? Should I have the kids work together in small groups or would it be better if I planned a whole-class discussion?"*

*Sam was surprised by Nick's questions and concerns. He knew that Nick liked math and especially liked teaching it. Nick had been really supportive to Sam at times, helping him plan particular lessons and swapping ideas and materials. He seemed so together when it came to math and didn't need to be nervous about the principal's observation. But Sam knew that Nick wanted to show his best, and he was willing to help.*

## 92 How can I plan for my principal's visit?

Having an administrator observe you can be an anxiety-producing experience. You want to do well, you want your students to do well, and you want your administrator to have confidence in your ability. Those are three big "wants." Because different administrators have different goals and expectations for classroom observations, it's important to have as clear a notion as possible of what your principal's purpose is before you plan for a visit.

For example, some principals see a classroom observation as a way to get a snapshot of your ability to teach math. For this purpose, your goal is to plan a lesson that shows your strengths and incorporates elements that you think are particularly important to your math instruction. Other principals, however, see a classroom observation as a time to give you help with something you've identified. In this case, you may want to teach a different sort of lesson, one that may feel a bit riskier. Also, while math is a strong area for some principals, it isn't everyone's area of expertise. This will have an effect on principals' points of view, on how they may interact with your students when they visit your class, and on the lesson you'll plan to teach.

For any point of view, however, it's important that you identify clearly the mathematics you plan to teach, the learning activities you'll introduce to help students interact with key ideas, what you'll expect students to do, and the indications you'll look for to determine whether the lesson was successful. The clearer you are, the better prepared the principal is for your classroom and the more specific your principal's feedback can be.

### 93 My administrator scheduled a visitation and we're in the middle of a unit and working on projects. I worry that the administrator won't see a "real" lesson. What can I do?

Keep in mind that your administrator has only a brief time in your classroom. Choose a lesson that has the best chance to show your capability as a math teacher, even if it's a lesson about which you have questions and would like feedback. Having the administrator observe students at work on projects may not serve this purpose. Of course, such a class may be testimony to your ability to set the stage for independent work, meet a variety of student needs, and engage students in mathematical investigations. It would give your adminstrator the chance to circulate and interact with students, something that might not be possible with a different lesson. If you have concerns that the visitation won't show your observer all that you'd like about your skills, that's probably a correct judgment.

It's fine to interrupt your overall plan and offer students a lesson that better typifies your teaching. Imagine someone is coming to dinner at your house on the spur of the moment. While you're a good cook and like to prepare for guests, this night you were planning just a salad for yourself and macaroni and cheese for the children. What do you do? You'd probably shelve your original plan and prepare something that's better suited for a company meal. Consider the same for an administrator's visit. You're not trying to do something dishonest by preparing a special lesson; you're putting your best effort into helping your observer understand how you teach math and how your students are learning math in your classroom.

## 94 I want to show my administrator how much my students know. What's the best way to do this?

The best way to show what your children know is to ask well-thought-out, pertinent questions and let your children respond. The questions themselves are the key to success. If you ask effective questions, ones that give children the chance to show how they think, reason, and use skills to solve problems, then your students will have the opportunity to communicate what they know. Good questions are indicators that you understand the mathematical purpose and goals of the lesson. Also, having a class discussion like this is useful for demonstrating your skill with teaching and with assessing students' understanding. Be sure to have a variety of questions prepared, more than you will probably need, to be sure that you'll be able to keep the conversation going. (*See page 33 for ideas about the role of questioning in the classroom.*)

Also, think about options for how you'll end the lesson. We know that one lesson isn't most often a self-contained experience in which students learn one specific idea; rather, it's part of a sequence of experiences that build understanding and skills. We also know that what happens in a lesson can determine what you'll do next. Your administrator needs to see how you use that particular day's lesson in relation to your overall instructional plans. With older students, think about ending your lesson by giving them a sense of what you learned from their participation. You might offer a preview of what they'll be doing the next day to give them some sense of continuity in their math learning. While it may not be appropriate to handle the end of class this way with younger students, be sure you communicate with the administrator what your lesson accomplished and what you plan to do next.

## 95 Is there anything I should avoid when my principal is observing me? If so, what?

Avoid trying a style that is entirely new either to you or to the children. When you're preparing for an observation, it's useful to ask a colleague for help with thinking of a strong lesson to use, one that will show your ability well. You'd like a lesson with a little extra pizzazz. But perhaps your colleague suggested a lesson that's a departure from your own style, that's different from what you ordinarily do in the classroom. If that's the case, you may not want to tackle it for the first time when an administrator is observing. Even though you may have planned well, your lack of experience could result in your being unprepared for surprises. When teaching something entirely new, you are dealing with many variables and you can get caught off guard. We realize that much of teaching calls for making on-the-spot decisions, but it's good to minimize the need for them during an observation.

You should also avoid using a great deal of the time having children work independently. If you include independent work, keep it short and be sure to devote time for students to share with the class. The administrator wants to see evidence of students' active engagement in your class. Plan a lesson that helps provide this evidence by involving the class in a discussion.

Also, avoid using manipulative materials that are new to the class. Remember that children's curiosity with new materials often makes it difficult for them to focus on the specific activity you have planned. Therefore, if you choose to use materials, make sure your students have sufficient prior experience so that they'll use them appropriately.

## 96  I made my lesson plan for the observation before I knew where my kids would really be mathematically, so my revised lesson won't match the plan I gave my administrator. What should I do now?

There are several possible reasons that your original plan is no longer suitable, causing you to revise your lesson plan. It may be because you had misjudged the progress the children would make by now and they don't have the prerequisite experience or skill for what you had originally planned. Or it may be that you progressed more quickly than you estimated and the lesson you planned is no longer appropriate.

If you submitted a lesson plan ahead of time, be sure to advise the administrator that your plans have changed. You don't want your observer to come to your classroom expecting to see one thing and become confused by seeing something else. Provide the change in plans in writing. Then, when you see your administrator at the post-observation conference, you can elaborate on your reason for changing. If you explain your rationale clearly, your administrator should understand.

## 97  What can I expect at the post-observation conference?

Your administrator will probably ask you to discuss your lesson, most likely reviewing with you your goals and the actual outcomes of the lesson. Your administrator may also point out portions of the lesson that were particularly effective. And finally, the administrator will offer recommendations—things that will make future lessons better. It's your administrator's job to help you grow. Even when lessons are beyond administrators' wildest dreams, they typically will offer you suggestions for improvement. Often these are observations that would have been hard for you to notice. It's difficult to be aware of everything in the classroom when you're actively teaching and especially hard with the added pressure of being observed; we all get nervous when someone is evaluating our performance. Also, you're so involved with the children that you can't see everything objectively. Your administrator's comments can offer you useful insights that weren't available to you before. Welcome them, reflect on them, and figure out how you can use them to improve your teaching. We can't grow unless we're willing to accept and act upon recommendations for improvement.

| **Thirteen** | *Making Plans for Substitutes* |

*It was the end of the day and Heather was exhausted and feeling sick. Several of her students were out with the flu, and now it seemed it was Heather's turn. "I can't be sick tomorrow!" she thought. "A sub will never be able to figure out how to do what I had planned for math." Heather needed to figure out what would be best for math class, but her head was pounding. She pulled out paper to write instructions.*

*While substitute teachers do their best with classes, there's no real substitute for a student's teacher, any more than there is a replacement for a parent. But it's inevitable that you'll need a sub for your class sometime during the year. The best time to plan is when you're healthy and alert, when you can think about alternatives for math lessons that will keep the students involved and learning and can also be successful for a substitute teacher.*

## 98 What can I do to set the scene for a substitute?

It's likely that you'll be absent sometime during the year, and it's good to plan ahead for the situation. This is easy if you know in advance when you'll be absent. But if you don't feel well when you wake up and have to call in sick, you're in no shape at that time to think about the day's lessons. Even if you keep detailed lesson plans in your desk, it's hard for a substitute who is unfamiliar with your class to understand your routines.

Our advice is to have information in place for substitutes that you've communicated to—and perhaps even created with—your students. Children are often uneasy in new situations and thinking in advance about working with a substitute can help them feel more comfortable. Both they and the substitute will be best supported if your expectations are clearly communicated. Also, a substitute will be more effective in your classroom if you've prepared your class ahead of time. One caution: Especially for younger children, allay concerns they may have about your being absent. Assure them that you're not planning on being sick, but that this is a "just in case" plan should you wake up some morning not feeling well and need to stay at home for a day.

Prepare a folder labeled "For the Substitute" and store it in a location that's easy to find. Include in the folder a cover letter, plans for the math the children are to do (*see page 118 for suggestions about this*), and an evaluation form for the substitute to complete. Older students should also know where the folder is kept and what's in it; for a younger class, it's better to ask the next-door teacher to help with this. Or perhaps your school has a system for this whereby every teacher has a sub folder on file in the office. Regardless, the idea is to involve the class as much as possible in welcoming a substitute and making the day's math lesson a success.

The cover letter should introduce your class to the substitute and provide information about how the students generally work during math time, routines that you follow, and logistics that may be useful. Involve your class in preparing this cover letter. With young children, lead a class discussion, write their ideas on chart paper, and transfer them later to the folder. With older students, this is a good assignment for groups to work on first and then discuss as a whole class. Either way will not only serve your substitute folder but also help you learn about how your students perceive the organizational structure of your class. If you use specific procedures for children to pair up or work in groups, make that clear. To help the substitute with using specific materials—manipulatives, markers, or scissors, for example—be sure that your cover letter includes information about where the materials are stored and how they are to be distributed and replaced.

Ask the substitute to record perceptions about the math activities and how they were received by the students. Ask for comments on how the children worked during math time. Invite her to note any observations she made while watching children work and share candidly any and all concerns. The substitute's written record serves as one tool you have for assessing the day's work in your classroom. As with the other information in the folder, students should have prior knowledge about what's asked for on the evaluation form. This helps them understand your expectations for them.

Consider having a "practice" substitute math class. Either invite someone to come to your class or pretend that you're the substitute. Ask the students for help figuring out what to do. They should guide you to the folder, help interpret its contents, and then get involved with the math you've planned.

## 99

**I worry that a substitute will have difficulty following my lesson plan or will confuse my students. Should I be concerned about this?**

A substitute won't teach exactly the way you do. Substitutes will certainly do their best to teach a new lesson, but it's difficult for someone else to step into your shoes. Even if you've left complete and detailed lesson plans, substitutes have their own teaching styles and previous experience. Also, you can't be completely sure that the lesson plans you left will communicate precisely enough or accomplish what you had hoped. Of course you're never positively sure that your plans will produce what you'd like, even when you're teaching. But at least then you have firsthand information about how to follow up in subsequent lessons. This reality makes it all the more important to have as much specific information as possible when you return about what occurred while you were out. (*See page 120 for suggestions about following up with your class on your return.*)

One strategy that we've found successful is to include activities in your substitute folder that you know will support your students' math learning, that the students will enjoy, and that are easy for the substitute to manage. Some teachers find that a selection of activities that reinforce learning is preferable to asking a substitute to teach something new. A substitute day is a perfect time to give children a chance to revisit ideas they've previously learned, and this approach will minimize confusion. Also, include information about whether the substitute should give the children a choice from the selection or should choose one activity for the entire class. If this idea makes sense to you, revisit the folder from time to time to make sure that the activities in it are still appropriate for your class.

## 100

**What are specific examples of learning activities that are good for substitute days?**

We find games to be useful learning tools throughout the year. Students enjoy them, and games provide practice with skills while also engaging students in reasoning and thinking strategically. There are always some games that become classroom favorites. But, as with toys, children lose interest in games as the year progresses. Also, as you move on to new topics, you'll drop some games taught earlier because they don't relate to the teaching you're currently doing. A substitute day is a good time to resurrect some of these games.

Many teaching resources offer appropriate math games and you probably have your favorites. The following suggestions offer models of games that we've found successful.

The Largest Wins is a game with many variations, depending on the skills appropriate for your students. For each, players use a die or a 0–9 spinner. Also, each player draws a game board (*see Figure 13–1*); the following examples show how the game can be tailored for different needs. Players take turns rolling or spinning and writing the number that comes up in one box. After all boxes are filled in, students do the calculation, if necessary, and compare to see who has the largest answer. The reject boxes are a way for students to try to avoid numbers that aren't helpful.

Note: Students can play the same game renamed as The Smallest Wins. The rules for play are the same, but the person with the lowest score is the winner. This switch calls for rethinking strategies and is a good challenge for students.

101 and Out requires a die or 0–9 spinner and works well for two, three, or four players. Each student makes a recording sheet. One player rolls the die or spins the spinner. All players write the number that comes up on the first line in either the tens column or the ones column. Then another player rolls or spins, and all players write the second number on the second line. Once players record a number, they can't

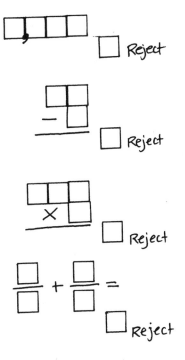

**13–1.** A variety of game boards makes playing The Largest Wins appropriate for different grade levels.

move it. Play continues for six numbers and the players then add. The student who has the sum closest to 100 without going over is the winner.

How Long? How Many? is a two-person game that calls for Cuisenaire rods, a sheet of centimeter-squared paper, and a die or 1–10 spinner. Students don't compete against each other in this game but play together to see how many squares they can cover. To play, they roll the die or spin the spinner twice. The first number tells "how long" a rod to use; the second number tells "how many" rods to take. They arrange the rods side by side to form a solid rectangle, trace the rectangle on the squared paper, and write the appropriate multiplication sentence inside. For example, rolling a 2 and then a 5 means players use the red 2-centimeter rods and take five of them; they arrange them into a two-by-five-centimeter rectangle and label if 2 × 5 = 10. Players take turns, one rolling or spinning and building the rectangle, and the other drawing and recording. But players should agree on where to place each rectangle on their paper. The game is over when they can't place a rectangle they've built. They figure out how many squares they've covered and how many are uncovered.

Our advice is to include in the substitute folder several games that the students are familiar with. They'll be eager for the day and will have the chance to revisit ideas and skills they've previously studied. If you'd prefer to include a new game, remember that the students should know what's in the folder, so tell them there will be a new game that you think they'll enjoy. This way they won't be caught off guard and be surprised—substitutes need as few surprises as possible to deal with. Or offer a new twist to games you've done previously with classes so that the versions in the folder feel fresh.

## 101  How should I follow up with the class after being absent?

Have a talk with the class and get the students' reactions to the math lesson they did with the substitute. Ask questions such as: "What did you do? What materials did you use? What worked well? What problems did you encounter? What improvements would you make to the folder? to the math activities?" Make an effort to get responses from a cross-section of your students so you have as accurate a picture of the day as possible. Or you might ask your students to write about what happened in math class when you were absent.

Also, read over the substitute's observations and comments about the day. Share them with your students so they have feedback from the substitute's point of view. And discuss the content of the work the children did. Review any written work that they did and discuss the results of their activities. Use these three pieces of data—a classroom follow-up discussion, the substitute's evaluation, and the children's written work—to determine changes you might make to your substitute system.

# Afterword

We suspect that *So You Have to Teach Math?* doesn't address all of your questions. We also suspect that reading our book will raise new questions for you. We're interested in hearing from you. If you think of questions that you wish we had included, please let us know. You can write or send an e-mail.

Write to:    Marilyn Burns and Robyn Silbey
               c/o Marilyn Burns Education Associates
               150 Gate 5 Road, Suite 101
               Sausalito, CA 94965

Send e-mail to: *MoreQuestions@mathsolutions.com.*